PHYSICS
PSYCHOLOGY AND
MEDICINE

PHYSICS PSYCHOLOGY AND MEDICINE

A Methodological Essay

BY

J. H. WOODGER, D.Sc.

*Professor of Biology in the
University of London*

CAMBRIDGE
AT THE UNIVERSITY PRESS
1956

PUBLISHED BY
THE SYNDICS OF THE CAMBRIDGE UNIVERSITY PRESS

London Office: Bentley House, N.W.1
American Branch: New York
Agents for Canada, India, and Pakistan: Macmillan

Printed in Great Britain by Jarrold & Sons Ltd., Norwich

To all Students of
MIDDLESEX HOSPITAL MEDICAL SCHOOL
this Essay is affectionately dedicated
by the author

Today he can discover his errors of yesterday and tomorrow he may obtain light on what he thinks himself sure of today.

From the Oath and Prayer of Maimonides, a Jewish physician of the twelfth century.

CONTENTS

PREFACE

THIS essay originated in three lectures given to staff and senior students of the physiology department of the Middlesex Hospital Medical School at the request of Professor Samson Wright. He asked me to lecture on the topics of Part III of my Tarner Lectures which were published in 1952 under the title *Biology and Language*. Part III dealt (among other things) with certain gaps in the medical curriculum and especially with the neglect of psychology in the education of doctors. In preparing this essay for publication at the suggestion of Professor Wright I have tried to repeat myself as little as possible, so that the interested reader will find these topics differently treated in the above book.

In this essay I have tried to devise a method of dealing with questions which are commonly regarded as controversial in as neutral a manner as possible. To some who take one side in these controversies much of what I have to say will seem platitudinous; to some who take the opposite side these same platitudes may seem to be the grossest heresies. I have addressed myself chiefly to those who are interested in finding where possible a middle position and especially to students and teachers who are still sufficiently unsophisticated to be neither bored by the platitudes nor shocked by the heresies.

Among the many friends and colleagues who kindly read this essay in manuscript I should like especially to mention my debt to Professors Sir Charles Dodds, John Gregg, R. O. Kapp and Samson Wright; also to Doctors George Day, John Klauber and Henry Yellowlees, to each of whom I am indebted for advice or encouragement. I would like to record my thanks to Miss Thornton, Secretary to the International Congress for Mental Health, for the loan of books and reports, and to my wife for help in proof-reading.

My thanks are also due to Dr George Day for permission for the quotation on p. 56; to Penguin Books, Ltd. for the passage from *Psychiatry Today*, by Dr D. Stafford-Clark; to the Commonwealth Fund and Harvard University Press for the quotation from *Public Health is People*, by Ethel Ginsberg; and to Secker and Warburg, Ltd. for permission to quote from *My Left Foot*, by Christy Brown.

J. H. W.

January 1956

§ 1. THE TRAINING OF A DOCTOR

In olden times a medical student would come into contact with patients even in his first year; he would be apprenticed to a surgeon or a physician and would accompany him on his rounds. But this system has long ago been abandoned. Medicine has now become scientific, but it is regarded as an applied science and so it is felt that the student must first be instructed in the basic sciences upon which all his future work will depend. When we look at the list of those basic sciences to which the work of the first year is devoted, we are astonished to find that not *one* of these sciences deals with human beings as persons or as members of societies. In other words no psychology or sociology is included. The only sciences taught as basic sciences are physics, chemistry and biology. Some people are even of the opinion that biology is superfluous, provided physics and chemistry are included.

The student is thus given a bias from the start. But perhaps this unfortunate result is soon corrected in the preclinical training. Unfortunately this is not so, at least in British universities. The effect of the preclinical training is all in the direction of reinforcing the impression left by the first-year studies. Anatomy is largely an affair of corpses that cannot talk. Physiology is frequently taught from the point of view of a dogma which has been expressed by William Bayliss in the following words: 'The aim of all physiological experimentation is to express vital processes in terms of physical and chemical laws. We call this "explaining" them.'

The student is thus taught to seek the living among the dead and so to regard human beings as complicated pieces of machinery whose parts can go wrong in various ways. But being miserable is not a recognized way in which a machine can go wrong. Its correction seems to call for a different approach. Nevertheless the attitude which has been inculcated in the preclinical period still largely dominates the clinical.

Writers on psychiatry sometimes complain of the prevailing canon of diagnosis which requires the 'exclusion of the organic' before a functional diagnosis is considered. Such authors point out that this results in some patients being unnecessarily subjected to many disagreeable tests. It may also have the result that some who are incorrectly diagnosed as organic may never have an opportunity of being diagnosed and treated as functional at all. This dichotomy and opposition of organic and functional, with the concentration of attention on the former, is just one aspect of the one-sided training of medical students.

There is no doubt that this training, based almost entirely on the physical sciences, has been successful, but we must not be so complacent as to allow this success to obscure other aspects of the situation. It has recently been stated in the House of Commons (19 February 1954) that 'out of 500,000 beds under the National Health Service, no fewer than 211,000 were for mental and mentally deficient cases'. This is a proportion of between two-fifths and one-half. Another authority has stated that 'the number of beds at present required for mental illness in all forms is approximately two-thirds of the total number required for all other forms of illness, accident and injury put together'. And 'these figures do not include the incidence of psychoneurotic illness among the general population, which has been calculated as a result of various surveys as falling somewhere between eight and eleven per thousand of the population'.* We thus have two states of affairs: a medical training which is overwhelmingly physical, and a sick population containing a high proportion of cases which are not classified as physical. The possibility suggests itself that this high proportion of mental illness may not be altogether unconnected with the lopsidedness of the doctor's training. Otherwise it would be surprising that a type of illness which occupies so little of the time of training should in fact form such a large proportion of all sick people. A consultant of the Tavistock Clinic, London, has recently stated:

It is generally agreed that at least one quarter of the work of the general practitioner consists of psychotherapy pure and simple. Some investigators put the figure at 50 per cent or even higher; but, whatever the figure may be, the fact remains that the present medical training does not properly equip the practitioner for at least one quarter of the work he will have to do.†

The type of training at present in use has other consequences connected with the fact that it tends to make students forget that they are dealing with persons. In a lecture on what he calls the Seven Sins of Medicine, by Dr Richard Asher,‡ it was stated that these sins include cruelty (and the author distinguished physical and mental cruelty) and bad manners. Such defects of conduct are

---

* Cf. also *The Lancet*, 14 August 1954, p. 324: 'In 1953 there were over 200,000 occupied beds in our overcrowded mental hospitals and mental-deficiency institutions, as against 212,000 occupied beds in hospitals for all other diseases put together. There is no field in medicine where research is so imperatively needed, and none so ill endowed.'

† M. Balint, 'Training general practitioners in psychotherapy', *British Medical Journal*, 16 January 1954, p. 115.

‡ *The Lancet*, 27 August 1949, p. 359. See also p. 54 below.

only to be expected if the underlying philosophy of medical education, at least during the preclinical years, encourages students to regard persons as automatic machines waiting for the penny to drop. Because many patients (perhaps most) in British hospitals do not like being treated as automatic machines. They want to be treated as persons. They will feel hurt and offended if they are not treated as sentient beings with feelings and pre-ferences.* If they are not treated as persons they may be-come unhappy and unresponsive to medical treatment. But surely it is the business of medicine to deal with human beings as they are in ordinary life, not as they would be if they conformed completely to this or that philosophical theory about them. No doubt from the point of view of the supporters of such philosophical theories the lack of con-formity of patients is deplorable, but medicine is an applied science not a purely theoretical one.

Some American universities seem to be much more enlightened than ours in these matters. Dr Muncie, in his *Psychobiology and Psychiatry* (1939), p. 17, writes: 'When the American Psychological Association in 1911 discussed the incorporation in the medical curricula of this country of some elementary facts concerning normal psychology, a momentous step in American medical education was instituted.' The proposal was put into effect at Johns Hopkins in 1913–14 and since then many other schools in the United States have followed this example.†

* As Dr Yellowlees has said: 'Never refer to a baby as "it" when talking to either of the parents—especially the mother.' *The Human Approach* (1946), p. 15.

† For an account of the provision now being made in many American medical schools for psychological teaching see *Psychiatry and Medical Education*, Report of the 1951 Conference on Psychiatric Education held at Cornell University, Ithaca, N.Y., 1951. The following remarks are illus-trative of the enlightened views on these topics now met with in the United States. Henry W. Wenk, pediatrician-psychiatrist in the University of

Although British medical schools are backward in these matters, a little historical research soon reveals that this is not for lack of good advice within our own shores. As long ago as 1935 there was issued the Report of the Conference of Representatives nominated by the Universities of Oxford, Cambridge and London, the Royal College of Physicians of London, the Royal College of Surgeons of England and the Society of Apothecaries of London. On p. 12 of this report we read:

The Conference suggests that a short course of lectures introductory to the psychological aspects of medicine should be given towards the end of the pre-clinical period. A suggested syllabus has been drawn up in Appendix C. Attendance at this course of lectures should be obligatory but no examination on their content should be held at this stage. It is believed that, if the lectures were given at convenient hours, they would be listened to with interest and constitute a useful introduction for the student to the psychological aspects of his future work as well as a contribution to his general education. Eight lectures, which should include advice in regard to the reading of books on the subject, should be sufficient for the purpose.

Louisville, said: 'My feeling is that the need is to get more of the knowledge of medical psychology into the other aspects of medical teaching. I feel that there is need for a basic course in psychology to complement the courses in physiology and biochemistry. I think that what is needed is a re-evaluation and reorganization of the entire medical curriculum in order to accomplish this purpose.' Dr Richard Wolf, a pediatrician of the Children's Hospital of Cincinnati, Ohio, said: 'I would like to contribute to the student's understanding of the child patient and his parents as people living in relationship with one another rather than regarding them as patients in a vacuum. To help get away from the idea that a comprehensive history is only to be taken by a psychiatrist and to enable the student to make a positive diagnosis of emotional difficulties rather than making one only by exclusion' (from *An Appraisal of Undergraduate Education in the United States, with reference to the Teaching of Psychology*, by Milton J. E. Sean, M.D., and Fred L. Stricker, M.D., mimeographed; issued by Yale University Child Study Centre).

On p. 15, referring to the clinical period we find the following:

It is highly important that the student should be made familiar with the psychological aspects of patients in the hospital, whether they are under treatment for organic disease or for functional nervous disorders, or are admitted merely for the purpose of observation and investigation.

So much for 1935. In 1944, nine years later, still nothing had been done, for we read on p. 18 of the report of the Planning Committee of the Royal College of Physicians of London on medical education the following:

In the medical curriculum the study of the mind is neglected, especially during the preclinical period, to the detriment of the future doctor. It is desirable that during the preclinical period time should be found for a short series of classes in psychology. . . . The exact nature of these classes is less important than their existence, for their function is to interest the student in psychology.

In the same year (1944) the report of the Inter-Departmental Committee on Medical Schools was issued by the Ministry of Health (it is commonly known as the Goodenough Report). On p. 184 we find:

It is undesirable for a student to be brought into contact with psychological illnesses until he knows something about the psychology of normal healthy persons. He should, therefore, be given a short elementary course of normal psychology during the pre-clinical part of this training, in association with the course in physiology.

Four years later the British Medical Association issued the report of its Medical Curriculum Committee under the title, *The Training of a Doctor*. This committee seems to have conducted its labours under the erroneous assumption

6

that the recommendation of its predecessors had been implemented, for this report refers to psychology as having 'only recently been added to the range of subjects to be studied in the pre-clinical period' (p. 46). The report therefore confines itself to a discussion of the form such instruction should take. On p. 94 it is stated that:

The Committee has already emphasized the importance of keeping before the student the mental as well as the physical aspects of health and disease. In his pre-clinical study of the normal human being he will have learned something of mental processes, and in his introduction to clinical medicine he will have been taught the principles of psychopathology.

On p. 96 we read:

The standard of training would be improved if general physicians would interest themselves more in the psychiatric aspects of illness. Too often in the past they have neglected in their medical teaching the psychological component of the patient's illness. This lack of interest, the absence of co-operation between the general physician and the psychiatrist, and the neglect of the valuable teaching material in the general medical and surgical wards, have been at least partly responsible for the unbalanced courses in psychological medicine, with their emphasis on psychotic conditions and clinical demonstrations in the mental hospital. It is not only with the general physician that the psychiatrist should co-operate . . . in almost every department of medical training opportunities may be found to demonstrate the psychological aspects of illness.*

* Occasionally we have an opportunity of learning something of the psychological side of illness from the patient's point of view. The following passages are from Christy Brown, *My Left Foot* (1954). The author suffered from cerebral palsy from infancy. 'We need confidence and friendliness as well as, if not more than, medical treatment. It is not only our muscles and limbs which bother us—sometimes it is our minds as well, our inner selves that require more attention than our twisted arms and legs. A child with a

We thus have the following extraordinary state of affairs:
at the present day (1955) no official teaching of psychological topics during the preclinical period in the medical
schools of the University of London, in spite of the fact
that authoritative reports issued at intervals of twenty,
eleven and seven years ago have all recommended that
provision for such teaching should be made. Under these
circumstances is it surprising that such a large proportion
of the available beds are occupied by mentally sick
patients?

But the situation is even more grave than it has so far
been depicted. Nothing has been said about school
education. Thanks to a tacit conspiracy between parents,
schoolmasters and universities, it is now possible for boys
and girls to abandon their general education before they
leave school, to telescope the beginnings of university
education back into the last years of school education.
They are now permitted to devote the last year or two
years of their school days to preparation for the First
M.B. examination, or for one which exempts them from
this one, thus enabling some of them to pass this examination before they enter the university. This means that they
begin the study of the physical sciences, when they mean
little more to them than extensions of play on the nursery

crooked mouth and twisted hands can very quickly and easily develop a set
of very crooked and twisted attitudes both towards himself and life in
general, especially if he is allowed to grow up with them without being
helped to an understanding of them. If the idea of his "difference" as compared to normal children is allowed to take root in his mind, it will grow
with him into adolescence and eventually into manhood, so that he will
look out on life with a mind as distorted as his body. Life becomes to him
just a reflection of his own "crookedness", his own emotional pain' (p. 160).
'My affliction was not, after all, "incurable". But something else was—
my lack of really "normal" human expression and relationship. No matter
how well I might conquer my handicap I would never be a normal individual
leading a normal life. The old "difference" would always remain. I wanted
so desperately to love and be loved . . .' (p. 141).

8

floor, at the expense of one or two years of study of the humanities, through which they might have learnt something about persons in preparation for dealing with persons in their capacity as doctors. Thus a bias in favour of the physical sciences is laid down even before the student enters the medical school.*

§ 2. REASONS FOR THE PRESENT STATE OF AFFAIRS IN MEDICAL EDUCATION

No doubt very many factors have contributed to bring about the state of affairs in medical education which has been depicted in the preceding section. In the following

---

* Although the above account of preclinical teaching is correct as far as official printed syllabuses are concerned, some unofficial effort is made in most schools in London to implement the reports quoted in the text. Of nine London institutions which provide for preclinical teaching one gives no lectures on psychology during the preclinical period, one gives four such lectures, one gives eight and one gives as many as ten, the remaining five schools each give six lectures. In one of these schools these lectures are given in the third term, in another in the term before that at the end of which the Second M.B. examination is held. In all the others the psychological lectures are given at the very end of the course when the students are all deeply engaged in their final revision for the Second M.B. examination, and are therefore in no mood to attend lectures on a new and (to one trained in the physical sciences) strange subject in which they will not be examined. In none of the schools mentioned is there any examination on the topics treated in the psychological lectures. When we contrast this meagre pittance of instruction in psychology, given at the end of the preclinical course, with the large share of time and care which is devoted to teaching the physical sciences, and when we recall the high proportion of patients who suffer from mental illness, it is difficult to believe that this treatment can enhance the importance of psychology in the minds of students, or encourage them to make themselves acquainted with it to the extent required by their future tasks. O monstrous! but one half-pennyworth of bread to this intolerable deal of sack!

pages I shall try to examine some of these factors, to discover any ill effects they may have had and to inquire how these are to be remedied. Perhaps the most important factor is the enormous and spectacular success of the physical sciences. This has resulted in a general lopsidedness of which that seen in medical education is only one example. It is partly responsible for the fact that we live in an age in which people are very clever in the management of gadgets but very helpless in the management of themselves, so that no one yet knows whether or not we shall blow ourselves to bits with the gadgets and so, by our own hands, end the episode of *Homo* (self-styled) *sapiens* on earth. But the effects of the success of the physical sciences are not only felt in the sphere of applications where they are most obvious, they extend into the realm of scientific theory and scientific method. In their most extreme form these effects find expression in the following doctrines: (i) that physical science is already able to supply all that is required in the way of explanatory hypotheses for any other science; and (ii) that for the successful development of any science all that is required is the faithful copying of the methods and application of the ideas of physics. Both of these doctrines seem to me to be pernicious for the following reasons. The first, if held dogmatically, would lead to the result that no new structures would be introduced into theoretical science; because it is equivalent to saying: 'Stop thinking, folks! The physicists have done all the thinking necessary.' Instead of letting the data suggest new ideas, it would mean that nothing new was admitted; everything would be shown to exemplify existing ideas. It would mean putting all our observational eggs into one theoretical basket; that is why the saying from William Bayliss quoted above is unfortunate. Moreover, this procedure would be in conflict with the second doctrine mentioned above. Because physics is and always has been free to go its own way, and it has shown a most admirable readiness both to abandon a cherished hypothesis when a better one has presented itself, and to vary its procedure when circumstances have required it. If, therefore, other sciences are to follow the procedure of physics, they too must be free to try any hypotheses which their data and their bright ideas may suggest, regardless of what other sciences may be doing; as well as to devise whatever procedural techniques may be suggested by their special problems. These remarks are not addressed to genuine applications of the physical sciences to other than their original fields. The sciences are characterized not so much by their special subject-matter as by their methods of abstraction and the theoretical apparatus which they bring to their tasks. For this reason biophysics is still physics and biochemistry still chemistry. The above remarks are aimed at the doctrine that all biology is either biophysics or biochemistry; that no new hypotheses are to be sought in biology other than those provided ready-made by physics and chemistry. Corresponding remarks apply to psychology and especially to medical psychology and its relation to neurology as a branch of physical science in the widest sense. In the field of medical psychology there is one and only one criterion of success, namely the restoration of patients to health. If a method or hypothesis helps us to do this, then it has nothing to fear, whatever may be said from the standpoint of neurology or physiology generally. Should anyone raise difficulties about the word 'health' in this formulation, one way of escape would be to let the patient himself be the arbiter. We might say that a patient is restored to health when he and his friends are satisfied with the results of his treatment and he ceases to consult a doctor. Like most formulations in this field this one will perhaps break down in special cases, but there is no law to compel a man to continue to consult a doctor.

Supposing this attitude to be approximately correct, we must now inquire how it comes about that medical men have been so dazzled by the brilliance of physics that they have thought it possible so far to neglect psychology. The physical sciences can be understood in two ways: (i) as a system of rules for manipulating the things we find in the world; and (ii) as a metaphysical doctrine about a world behind the scenes of ordinary life. Now the overwhelming success of the physical sciences under the first aspect has generated a widespread belief in the metaphysical doctrine under the second aspect, and it is very largely the unacknowledged influence of this belief which has been so unfavourable to the development of psychological medicine. Usually these two aspects of the physical sciences are not sharply distinguished nor the different criteria for judging them clearly understood; from this it has resulted that the claims of the second have often appeared to be stronger than they are, on account of the reflected glory of the first in which they have shone. It is not difficult to understand why this is so, and also why it is not more widely recognized. This we can do if we are prepared to recognize *another* gap in the education of medical students. This is one which they share with science students in general. This gap arises from the fact that although these students are taught a lot of science of various kinds they are not taught anything *about* science; they are not taught anything of the anatomy and physiology of science itself. This gap in the medical curriculum was recognized in the report already mentioned of the medical curriculum committee of the British Medical Association, § 51 of which is as follows:

The fundamental purpose of the course in the basic sciences is to teach scientific method and to inculcate clear and logical thinking. The scientific approach should be quite deliberately taught; it cannot be acquired as a by-product of factual instruction. This involves the training of the student in the importance of unprejudiced observation and of controlled experiment, in the evaluation of evidence and in the role of techniques and their limitations. *The student should also be disciplined in the proper use and meaning of words and the relationship of names and words to ideas and things.* At the end of the year's course he should have acquired a scientific attitude of mind and have absorbed in that attitude the atmosphere of unbiased inquiry and research.*

This is clearly a counsel of perfection and since the teachers are themselves victims of this gap it is difficult to see how the above recommendation is to be carried out in practice until teachers have been specially trained. It is the object of the next six sections of this essay to provide the reader with information which will enable him to estimate better the status of scientific doctrines and their bearing on the difficulties of medical psychology.

§ 3. DOGMATISM AND SCEPTICISM

To be dogmatic or to be sceptical is to take a certain attitude towards a statement or set of statements. To take a sceptical attitude is to take an attitude of doubting towards a statement, and to be dogmatic is to take an attitude devoid of all doubt, and of unwillingness to admit of any doubt, towards a statement which cannot be *known* to be true, that is to say, towards a statement regarding

* Italic not in text.

which we are not in a position to say that at no future date will it require or undergo revision.

Being sceptical towards a statement does not mean rejecting it outright. That would be dogmatic if the statement is of the kind towards which a dogmatic attitude is possible. Being sceptical means taking an attitude of suspended judgment between the extremes of dogmatic acceptance and dogmatic rejection.

Dogmatism and scepticism, like sin, are both widely condemned and widely practised. We all know the man who is passionately convinced that his views are the true ones, and we know his counterpart in another camp who is equally convinced about *his* views, diametrically opposed and contradictory though they may be to those of the first. It rarely occurs to either side that both *may* be wrong and (if they are contradictory) both *cannot* be right. Natural science is traditionally supposed to be free from dogmatism. But as it is persons, not sciences, that are dogmatic, and as persons do not cast off all the peculiarities of mankind when they become men of science, it would not be surprising if occasionally men of science were to be found who take a dogmatic attitude towards some statements—even towards statements belonging to natural science.

Among the sources of dogmatism in science may be mentioned success, explaining away and ignorance. Many scientific doctrines have been extremely successful and, although success and truth are not co-extensive (as we see from the way in which successful doctrines have been replaced by still more successful ones), nevertheless, success generates feelings of confidence and of infallibility which are often difficult to resist. In the writing of popular and school science, where too much qualification of the statements would be confusing and out of place, it is especially difficult to avoid dogmatism.

On the whole, persons tend to believe what they want to believe* and dogmatism may be the result of the practice of explaining away unfavourable observations in order to be able to continue to maintain a favourite doctrine. This practice is widespread and will be discussed in more detail in later sections.

Ignorance, in the learned world of today, is inevitable and therefore excusable. Daily we all become *relatively* more ignorant, because every day the world's presses pour forth a flood of articles, monographs and books in such quantity that no one can hope to read, still less to study critically and assimilate, more than a fraction even of that part which concerns him. Ignorance as a source of dogmatism is especially insidious in science, because the classification and mutual relations of statements are involved and, as we saw at the end of the last section, these are topics upon which men of science and, in particular, medical students, do not receive systematic or very up-to-date instruction. We must consider therefore the classification of scientific statements, and, as a preliminary to this, we must devote a little time to considering the basic requirements of science.

§4. SOME BASIC REQUIREMENTS OF SCIENCE

IT is often said that science is based upon observation and experiment. It might even be said that science consists of

---

* On p. 75 of her biography of Sir Winston Churchill, 1953, Virginia Cowles writes (quoting Sir Winston's own book *My Early Life*): 'I adopted quite early in life a system of believing what I wanted to believe, while at the same time leaving reason to pursue unfettered whatever paths she was capable of treading.'

the records of observations and of rules for doing all manner of things based upon such records. But the situation is in fact much more complicated than this saying suggests. I shall pick out three basic requirements for consideration: (i) bright ideas; (ii) observations (with or without experimentation); and (iii) apparatus.

The making of observations is not an entirely random process. It is always conducted under the guidance, more or less remote, of ideas, more or less bright. Moreover, observations are fleeting experiences. They fade rapidly in the memory and are lost forever if they are not *recorded* in some way. We therefore need an *apparatus for recording* observations, and this is usually provided by written statements which I shall call *observation records*.

Observation records are *singular* statements, that is to say they are records of particular observations of particular things in particular places at particular times. They are mostly found in note-books rather than in printed books. This is because the observation records which are needed in natural science are those which can be successfully *generalized*, and it is in fact the statements which result from such a generalizing process that we usually find in scientific literature. Thus William Harvey, having observed in certain particular instances that the systole of the heart in vertebrate animals is followed or accompanied by diastole of the arteries, says nothing about these particular instances in his book. He simply writes: *Whenever the heart is in systole the arteries are in diastole*; and this is a perfectly general statement which makes no mention of particular instances. It is moreover a *universal* general statement, because it asserts something about *all** hearts in systole, not only about some hearts. If I say:

Some patients recover after treatment with quinine

* All hearts, that is to say, which are connected with arteries.

I again have a statement which does not explicitly refer to particular instances and is therefore a general statement, but it is called an *existential* general statement to distinguish it from general statements of the first kind.

It is clear that universal generalizations of observation records say much more than the observation records which suggest them, or are made subsequently in confirmation of them, except in the comparatively trivial case where the possible instances are identical with the actual observed instances. Ordinarily such generalizations cover a vast range of instances, past, present and future, most of which are inaccessible to us. In the sense that such statements thus *go beyond* observation they are *hypothetical*. Consequently such generalizations provide an instance of a type of statement regarding which it is possible to be dogmatic. We cannot be *certain* that such generalizations will always continue to hold good in the future. The process of passing from a few observation records to a universal generalization thereof may therefore properly be called *guessing*. In the biological sciences and in psychology it is a somewhat hazardous undertaking and its results frequently require qualification or other forms of revision. A striking example of this is provided by the recent discovery of fishes in Antarctic waters which are devoid of haemoglobin.

The reverse process of passing from universal general statements to singular statements can only be accomplished with the help of another singular statement. Thus from the two statements,

(i) All human beings have red blood corpuscles,
(ii) Mr Smith is a human being,

I can obtain the further singular statement,

(iii) Mr Smith has red blood corpuscles.

The two kinds of general statement so far mentioned are of the form 'All Xs are Ys', in the one case, and 'Some Xs are Ys' in the other. These can be regarded as special cases of a more general form of statement, namely:

$$x \text{ per cent of } X\text{s are } Y\text{s.}$$

If we substitute '100' for 'x' in this expression we obtain '100 per cent of Xs are Ys' and this is another way of saying that all Xs are Ys. It will be noticed that it is only from statements of the 'All Xs are Ys' type that we can derive a singular statement with the help of another singular statement in the way explained above. Apart from this there seems to be no fundamental difference between the general type 'x per cent of Xs are Ys' and the special case 'All Xs are Ys.' In *both* cases the general statement is based upon the examination of a *sample* and, in so far as it goes beyond any particular sample, it is a hypothesis. For reasons which will soon become apparent I sometimes refer to such statements as 'zero-level hypotheses'.

When we have accumulated a number of such universal generalizations of observation records the question will suggest itself: Can we find a still more general statement from which all these generalizations will *follow* as *logical consequences*? It is here that bright ideas come once more into the picture. From time to time gifted people have bright ideas which suggest how such more general statements may be formulated. I shall call such more general statements *explanatory hypotheses of the first order or level*. I call them this because at a later stage, when a number of such explanatory hypotheses have been obtained, it may be possible to formulate yet another still more general statement from which all the first-order explanatory hypotheses follow as logical consequences. This would be an explanatory hypothesis of the second order or level. In this way, in the theoretically more advanced sciences, many layers of explanatory hypotheses have in the course of time been built up.

It is important to notice and bear in mind the distinction between generalizations of observation records (or zero-level hypotheses) and explanatory hypotheses. The former *say more* than the observation records that suggest them, but only in the sense that they are more general and involve unobserved instances, not in the sense that they introduce any new notion. We merely pass from some to all. But the introduction of a successful explanatory hypothesis usually requires the introduction of a new unifying idea. It involves what may be called *changing the subject*, because the new explanatory hypothesis speaks about something which was not mentioned in the generalizations that are among its consequences. In genetics, for example, on zero level we speak of classes of parents, of offspring and of environments, which are involved in breeding experiments. The first-level hypotheses speak about classes of gametes, classes of zygotes formed by the union of these gametes in pairs, and the development of these zygotes into adults in environments of various kinds. Explanatory hypotheses thus often speak of things which are not observed in the sense in which the things spoken of in the zero-level hypotheses are observed. In the genetical example, observation by the microscope is involved and hence the hypotheses of optical theory are also involved.

A good explanatory hypothesis is expected to have a much wider spread of consequences than the generalizations or zero-level hypotheses which it was introduced to cover. The wider the spread of consequences the more fruitful the hypothesis will be. Because, in so far as an explanatory hypothesis speaks about unobservable things, it cannot itself be directly tested by observation, but only through its logical consequences on the observational level. A hypothesis with a wide spread of consequences will therefore stimulate the search for confirmatory consequences over a wide area and will therefore be more likely to lead to new discoveries.

According to the above view of the matter, explanatory hypotheses are thought of as being chiefly aids to discovery, but they also have a classificatory function. They provide ways of grouping together zero-level statements, which would otherwise be unrelated and unmanageable. But some people regard explanatory hypotheses as revelations of another world behind the scenes of the observational level. This brings us back to the two aspects of the physical sciences which were mentioned earlier (p. 12). We can say now that there are two ways of looking at explanatory hypotheses in natural science and these we may call the pragmatic and the metaphysical. According to the pragmatic view these hypotheses help us in the mastery of the physical world—they lead us to manipulate the things of that world in ways which would not be thought of without their aid; they have led to the invention of new machines, to the synthesis of new substances, and to ways of eliminating diseases, and so on. According to the metaphysical view they do this because they reveal the secrets of a world behind the scenes. Everyone can check for himself the claims of the pragmatic view. The metaphysical view cannot be checked and so remains the battleground for interminable disputes. This will be further explained later.

We have now seen some of the ways in which bright ideas enter into the development of a science. Science *without* bright ideas has been called *scientism*. In connexion with psychology it has recently been vividly described in the following terms:

> Scientism is to science as the Pharisee is to the man of God. In the psychology of scientism there is everything to impress the onlooker—enormous libraries, and a systematic search of the journals, expensive instruments of exquisite precision and shining brass, complicated formulas, multi-dimensional geometries and differential equations, long strange words of Greek origin, freshly minted, enormous calculating machines and white-coated girls to punch them—all the equipment is there to make the psychologist feel that he is being really scientific—everything in fact except ideas and results. Full many a glorious thesis have I seen wending its dignified way to a trivial and predestined inconclusion, armed cap-à-pie with all the trappings of scientism; the decimals correct, the references in order, only the mind lacking.*

Of our three basic requisites—bright ideas, observations and apparatus—little has so far been said about apparatus. We have spoken only about *linguistic* apparatus —that part of our apparatus which is essential for recording observations, for formulating generalizations of such records and for giving expression to explanatory hypotheses. We shall have more to say about this linguistic apparatus presently; meanwhile a few words must be devoted to apparatus for *making* observations. In the course of the development of natural science—especially of the physical sciences—the explanatory hypotheses which have been introduced have suggested the invention of new apparatus for making observations. Physics has presented medicine with microscopes, thermometers and X-ray machines—to mention only a few. The observations made with the new apparatus have in turn suggested new hypotheses in the course of time. In this way the

* Bernard Notcutt, *The Psychology of Personality* (1953), p. 4.

structure of science becomes increasingly complicated and the testing of hypotheses increasingly difficult on account of the complicated connexions which these new hypotheses will have with the observation records. As we have already mentioned in connexion with the microscope, observation records got with the new apparatus will depend for their interpretation upon the theory of the apparatus, i.e. upon the explanatory hypotheses which led to its invention and construction. We have thus reached a point in our argument when it is essential to have an understanding of the relation between explanatory hypotheses and the generalizations of observation records upon which the testing of the former depends. This is the relation of *following from* or *logical consequence of*.

§ 5. THE CONSEQUENCE RELATION

THE notion of logical consequence has several times been referred to. In passing from observation records to generalizations thereof, and from thence to explanatory hypotheses of various orders, we proceed by guessing—if possible by inspired guessing, especially where explanatory hypotheses are concerned. In passing in the opposite direction—from the more general to the less general, and finally from the general to the particular, we make use of the relation of logical consequence between statements. This use of the word 'consequence' in connexion with statements should not be confused with its use in connexion with events, as when we say that vomiting is a consequence of swallowing an emetic.

Ordinarily the passage in either direction is performed

intuitively and almost automatically and so little attention is paid to it, except in such a science as physics in which mathematics is explicitly used to work out the consequences of hypotheses. In other sciences the degree and manner in which the passage in one direction differs from that in the other tends to be overlooked, and this situation is perpetuated by the prevailing unfortunate habit of using a common terminology for the passage in *both* directions. Thus the words 'inference', 'proof', 'conclusion', 'demonstration' and even 'deduction' are frequently, but unwittingly, used in two totally different senses. This is a potent but unrecognized source of misunderstanding, of dogmatism and of the misuse of science.

The only way out of all this confusion is through an understanding of the consequence relation. In order to get some notion of this relation we must first examine some simple examples of the construction of statements, because it is upon the construction of statements that the consequence relation depends.

For example, if we take any statement, such as

$$\text{Tom is bald,} \qquad \text{(A)}$$

it is possible to construct another statement by inserting the word '*not*' into it in accordance with the rules of English grammar, obtaining

$$\text{Tom is } not \text{ bald.} \qquad \text{(B)}$$

These two statements are such that if one is true the other must be false.* The second is called the *negation* of the first. If we found two statements related to one another in this

---

* This point is sometimes obscured and confused with a different one on account of the occurrence of vague words in the statements concerned. Thus someone might say 'I would not call Tom bald', while another would be willing to agree that Tom was bald. Then someone may say that statement (A) is neither true nor false. Such difficulties are overcome in science by

way in the same book we should feel that there had been some mistake. We should feel that we had been given no information on the matter at all, because we should not know which of the two statements was expressing the author's intentions.

Another way of constructing statements is by joining two together. If I join two statements together by the word 'and' I obtain a new statement called their *conjunction*, thus,

Paris is in France *and* Rome is in Italy.   (C)

This will be true only when *both* of the two constituent statements are true. If, therefore, I join two statements, one of which is the negation of the other, by 'and' I must get a statement which is false *whatever* statement I choose. Thus the conjunction of (A) and (B) above must be false and so is

Paris is in France *and* Paris is *not* in France.

Any statement which is false in this way, irrespective of its subject-matter, but simply because it involves both the affirmation and the denial of something, is called a *contradiction*.

It will be seen that the conjunction of

Paris is *not* in France

with the statement (C) above is a contradiction and we shall see that for this reason the statement

Paris is in France

is a logical consequence of (C). We can in fact adopt the

laying down more or less arbitrary definitions. For example, we might agree that a person is bald if he has *less than* 100 hairs on his head (exclusive of eyelashes, eyebrows, moustache and beard). Then in any given case a man either does or does not have less than 100 hairs and so either (A) or (B) is true but not both.

following as a criterion of whether a statement follows from another. We can say

One statement is a consequence of or follows from another if the conjunction of the latter with the negation of the former is a contradiction.

Another way of joining two statements to construct a third is by means of the word '*or*'; for example,

Paris is in France *or* Rome is in Italy

is such a compound and is called a *disjunction* or *alternation*. It will be true (in the sense of '*or*' here intended) if at least *one* of the two constituent statements is true, and false if both are false and only if both are false.

Now let us see what happens when we form the disjunction of a statement with its own negation, e.g.

Tom is bald *or* Tom is *not* bald.

As the two statements here joined by '*or*' are negations of one another, one must be true and therefore the conditions for the truth of the disjunction are satisfied. Such a disjunction will therefore be true whatever the statement chosen. A statement which is true in this way independently of the subject-matter of the constituent statements is said to be *logically true*. It can be shown that the negation of a contradiction is a logically true statement.

If we construct a disjunction from the negation of one statement with another statement, e.g.

Paris is *not* in France *or* Rome is in Italy,

we obtain a statement which is true except when the left-hand statement is true and the right-hand one is false. Thus

Paris is *not* in France *or* Rome is in Spain

is false because Paris is in fact in France and Rome is not

25

in Spain. A statement having such truth-conditions is sometimes written

> *If* Paris is in France *then* Rome is in Italy,

so that

> *If* Paris is in France *then* Rome is in Spain

is false. A statement written in this form is called a *conditional* statement, the left-hand component being called its *antecedent* and the right-hand component its *consequent*.

This provides us with another way of formulating a criterion for deciding when one statement is a consequence of another. We can say

> *One statement is a consequence of another statement if the conditional having the latter as its antecedent and the former as its consequent is logically true.*

In order to provide an example of the use of this criterion we can consider the following three statements:

The night is cloudless	(D)
Venus is visible	(E)
If the night is cloudless *then* Venus is visible.	(F)

Our problem is to discover whether (E) follows from the conjunction of (D) and (F). In the terms of our second criterion this means that we must inquire whether the conditional

> *If* [(D) *and* (F)] *then* (E)

is logically true. And since (F) is itself a conditional having (D) as antecedent and (E) as consequent we can also say that our problem is to determine whether

> *If* {(D) *and* [*if* (D) *then* (E)]} *then* (E)

is logically true. This is easily decided. For if (D) and (E) are both true then the conjunction of (D) and (F) is true and the conditional with this as antecedent and (E) as consequent will be true. If (D) is false and (E) true, then the conjunction of (D) with (F) will be false and, (E) being true, the conditional with that conjunction as antecedent and (E) as consequent will be true. Again, suppose (D) is true and (E) is false. Then the conditional (F) will be false and so the conjunction of (D) with (F) will be false and we shall have the major conditional with both antecedent and consequent false and so it as a conditional will be true. Finally suppose (D) and (E) are both false. Then again the conjunction of (D) with (F) will be false and so the conditional having this conjunction as antecedent and (E) as consequent will be true. Thus under each of the four possible distributions of truth and falsehood between (D) and (E) the conditional as a whole comes out true. It is therefore logically true and so (E) follows from the conjunction of (D) with (F). We can generalize this result as follows: we can say

> From the conjunction of a conditional with its own antecedent its consequent always follows.

Moreover it will be seen that when the antecedent and the conditional are both true the consequent must also be true. In other words our rule is such that it leads from true premisses to true conclusions.

It can be left as an exercise for the reader to show that the same result is obtained by our first criterion, i.e. to show that

$$(D) \text{ and } (F) \text{ and not } (E)$$

is a contradiction.

Next we have to show that from

> *If* the night is cloudless *then* Venus is visible   (F)

and   Venus is visible   (E)

it is not possible to infer

The night is cloudless.   (D)

The simplest way to show this will be by showing that the conjunction

(E) *and* (F) *and not* (D)

is *not* a contradiction. This is important both for understanding the status of explanatory hypotheses in science and also because it is not an uncommon mistake among students to suppose that it is possible to infer the antecedent of a conditional if we are given the conditional and its consequent. Returning to our example we proceed as follows: First suppose that (D) is false and (E) is true; then the conditional (F) (which is: if (D) then (E)) will be true and the negation of (D) will be true. Therefore the conjunction of (E) with (F) and the negation of (D) will be true and so cannot be a contradiction. Consequently (D) does not follow from the conjunction of (E) and (F). In other words from

Venus is visible

and

If the night is cloudless *then* Venus is visible

we cannot infer

The night is cloudless.

One more technical point must be explained before we can proceed with our main theme. If we are given a conditional

if (A) *then* (C),   (1)

where (A) is the antecedent and (C) the consequent, then

it is always permissible to transform it into another conditional namely

$$\text{if not (C) then not (A)} \tag{2}$$

and it will be found that (2) follows from (1). In other words we can reverse the order of antecedent and consequent in a conditional *provided* we first negate them both. The resulting conditional will be true if the original one was true and false if the original one was false. This is called the *law of transposition*.

We are now in a position to say something more precise about the relations between the various types of statement in scientific theories and about the testing of explanatory hypotheses. Suppose that '*H*' is an explanatory hypothesis and '*G*' is one of the zero-level generalizations that are among the consequences of '*H*'. This will mean, as we can now see, that the conditional

$$\text{if } H \text{ then } G \tag{i}$$

is logically true. What must we do in order to test '*H*'? We must make a prediction from '*G*' and then make the appropriate observations to see whether this prediction is correct. But we have already seen that it is impossible to derive a singular statement (such as a prediction is) from a generalization alone, but only from a generalization in conjunction with another singular statement. Suppose, then, that S_1 and S_2 are singular statements (S_1 being an observation record) and that

$$\text{if } (G \text{ and } S_1) \text{ then } S_2 \tag{ii}$$

is logically true so that S_2 follows from the conjunction of S_1 and G. If we now make the appropriate observation and find that this agrees with S_2 (i.e. prediction and observation agree), then we can say that so far as this observation goes the hypothesis 'H' from which S_2 follows by way of the conjunction of 'G' with 'S_1' (an observation record) is confirmed. We cannot say that this observation S_2 shows the hypothesis 'H' to be true, because, as we have already explained, we cannot from a conditional and its consequent infer its antecedent. However many times our predictions are confirmed by our observations we cannot say that the hypothesis concerned *follows from* these observations.

But suppose that our observation *contradicts* our prediction, so that 'not S_2' instead of 'S_2' is a true observation record. Then we proceed as follows. First we apply the law of transposition to our last statement (ii) and obtain

$$\text{if not } (S_2) \text{ then not } (G \text{ and } S_1). \qquad \text{(iii)}$$

As this is a conditional of which we are supposing that we already have the antecedent we can infer its consequent

$$\text{not } (G \text{ and } S_1). \qquad \text{(iv)}$$

From this by means of what is called de Morgan's law which the reader can easily check for himself, we can obtain

$$\text{not } (G) \text{ or not } (S_1), \qquad \text{(v)}$$

which can also be written

$$\text{not } (S_1) \text{ or not } (G), \qquad \text{(vi)}$$

and this, as we have learnt, can be written as a conditional

$$\text{if } S_1 \text{ then not } (G). \qquad \text{(vii)}$$

Once more we have a conditional and its antecedent (since we are assuming that S_1 is a true observation record) and so we can infer its consequent

$$\text{not } (G). \qquad \text{(viii)}$$

We now apply the principle of transposition to our statement (i) and obtain

$$\textit{if not } (G) \textit{ then not } (H) \qquad\qquad (\text{ix})$$

and from (viii) and (ix) we finally get

$$\textit{not } (H). \qquad\qquad (\text{x})$$

This means that although 'H' does *not* follow from the discovery of 'S_2', the negation of 'H' *does* follow from the discovery of the negation of 'S_2'. When therefore 'not S_2' is obtained by observation it would seem that we must automatically reject 'H'. But this is by no means what always happens. If 'H' is not a well-established hypothesis, little difficulty will be felt about rejecting it. But if 'H' is a well-established hypothesis, then recourse is usually had to a process of *explaining away* in order to save it. Thus doubts may be cast upon S_2. But if repetitions of the observations always give the same result this method will in the long run be abandoned. An alternative will then be to introduce a supplementary hypothesis which will satisfactorily explain why the expected result is not obtained and so enable us still to retain 'H'. Thus the refutation of an explanatory hypothesis is not always a simple matter.

A particularly striking example of explaining away is provided by the way in which the doctrine of preformation was maintained in the early days of the study of animal development. Some biologists were prepared to accept development as a process to be investigated. The preformationists, however, insisted upon explaining it away by asserting that the observed development was illusory because the adult structures were already present, in miniature, from the start. The fact that they were not observed was explained away by the simple assertion that they were invisible. This is a good example of bolstering up a hypothesis by means of a subsidiary hypothesis. But the preformationists did not call it this. They called it the Triumph of Reason over the Senses (in the true Platonic tradition).*

§ 6. THE STATUS OF EXPLANATORY HYPOTHESES

WE have now distinguished *four* kinds of statement occurring in natural science: (i) observation records; (ii) generalizations of observation records; (iii) explanatory hypotheses (of various orders); and (iv) consequences of explanatory hypotheses other than those under (ii). It has already been pointed out that it is not possible to be *certain* that a given generalization of observation records is true when (as is usually the case) it covers instances which are not accessible to observation. Regarding such statements it is therefore possible to be dogmatic. We now see that the same also applies to explanatory hypotheses, although for a different reason. Such statements can only be tested indirectly through their consequences. A conditional statement is thus involved with the explanatory hypothesis as antecedent, and we have just seen that from a true conditional we cannot infer the antecedent if we are given the consequent. It is therefore erroneous and most misleading to speak of *verifying* an explanatory

* For a detailed account of this interesting episode in the history of embryology see F. J. Cole's *Early Theories of Sexual Generation* (1930). This author's moralizing about Malpighi (p. 48), 'a man who could see one thing and believe another', fails to take account of the fact that the preformation doctrine did not claim to be a generalization of observation records but an explanatory hypothesis. Everyone who believes in the atomic hypothesis may be said to see one thing and believe another.

hypothesis. However many times observations may confirm the predictions of such a hypothesis, this does not entitle us to say that the hypothesis is true; although when a hypothesis is successful it is difficult not to believe that it is true. We can only say, as we can about a successful generalization of observation records, that so far it has not been contradicted. Like the generalizations which follow from them, explanatory hypotheses are at the mercy of future observations. Nevertheless, as we saw at the end of the last section, when a hypothesis has been contradicted by observation records it is always possible, for a time at least, to bolster it up by recourse to the process of explaining away the unfavourable observation records with the help of subsidiary hypotheses. In this connexion the following remarks of Lord Russell are interesting:

A hypothesis should accord with all known relevant observations, and suggest experiments (or observations) which will have one result if the hypothesis is true and another if it is false. This is an ideal: in actual fact, other hypotheses will always exist which are compatible with what is meant to be an *experimentum crucis*. The crucial character can only be as between *two* hypotheses, not as between one hypothesis and all the rest. . . . The argument in favour of a theory is always the formally invalid argument: 'p implies q, and q is true, therefore p is true.' Here p is the theory and q is the observed relevant facts.*

In another place Lord Russell writes:

We can construct theories which fit the known facts, but we can never be sure that other theories would not fit them equally well. This is an essential limitation to scientific inference which

---

* *Analysis of Matter* (1927), p. 194. By 'p implies q' Lord Russell means what has here been called 'if p then q' ('p' and 'q' represent any statements). Note that the relation between hypothesis and observation record is rather more complicated than it is here represented by Lord Russell.

is generally recognized by men of science; no prudent man of science would maintain that such-and-such a theory is so firmly established that it will never call for modification.*

Yet another aspect of the question is touched upon by Lord Russell in the following passage:

what is surprising in physics is not the existence of general laws, but their extreme simplicity. It is not the uniformity of nature that should surprise us, for, by sufficient analytical ingenuity, any conceivable course of nature might be shown to exhibit uniformity. What should surprise us is the fact that the uniformity is simple enough for us to be able to discover it. But it is just this characteristic of simplicity in the laws of nature hitherto discovered which it would be fallacious to generalize, for it is obvious that simplicity has been a part cause of their discovery, and can therefore give no ground for the supposition that other undiscovered laws are equally simple.†

It is curious in this connexion to recall one of the conditions which Stanley Jevons supposed a good explanatory hypothesis should satisfy. He wrote:

(2) That it do not conflict with any laws of nature, or of mind, which we hold to be true.‡

It is plain that if physicists had followed this rule there would have been little or no development of physical theory and Einstein's doctrines would never have been allowed to challenge those of Newton.

It is abundantly clear from all the foregoing that explanatory hypotheses are statements of the kind about which it is possible to be dogmatic, and that we should not expect 'the prudent man of science' to be dogmatic about

* *Analysis of Matter* (1927), p. 255.

† *Scientific Method in Philosophy* (Oxford, 1914), p. 8. Note that the simplicity referred to is absent in the biological sciences.

‡ *The Principles of Science* (1900), p. 511.

them. This is further reinforced by a study of the history of natural science. From such a study we learn, among other things, the following:

(i) That new explanatory hypotheses are often violently opposed, or completely ignored, when they are first proposed.

(ii) That when a new explanatory hypothesis has a wider umbrella of consequences than existing ones in the same field it will in time prevail and finally become accepted. ('In time' here means when sufficient time has elapsed for all those to have died off who have a vested interest in condemning the new hypothesis.)

(iii) That new successful hypotheses may themselves be permitted in time to harden into dogmas (except among the prudent!) and so to become barriers to further developments.

(iv) That as we do not know which of our existing hypotheses will at some future date be replaced by new ones, we do not know which of them are true.

(v) That a hypothesis can be useful even when it is not true (i.e. truth and success are not coextensive); because hypotheses which have been superseded are often still useful within the field for which they were originally devised (e.g. Newtonian mechanics).

A. N. Whitehead, in his *Principle of Relativity* (1922), in describing what he called 'the habitual working gauge of science', wrote: 'Only one question is asked: Has the doctrine a precise application to a variety of particular circumstances, so as to determine the exact phenomena which should then be observed? In the comparative absence of these applications beauty, generality, or even truth, will not save a doctrine from neglect in scientific thought.'

It seems clear from all that has been said above that the procedure of natural science begins and ends with observations (with or without experimentation). If explanatory hypotheses tell us about the secrets of an unobservable world behind the scenes, as some people have believed, then there seems to be no way of discovering whether what they tell us is true. The part which explanatory hypotheses play in natural science has already been suggested. We have mentioned that they have a classificatory function, by grouping together large numbers of generalizations of observation records and thus making them more manageable. But their most important function seems to be in going beyond these generalizations and suggesting hitherto unsuspected directions in which to pursue observation and experiment. This is seen especially clearly when an explanatory hypothesis leads to the invention of a new apparatus for observation. Whitehead again expresses the situation very well when he says:

The true method of discovery is like the flight of an aeroplane. It starts from the ground of particular observation; it makes a flight in the thin air of imaginative generalization; and it again lands for renewed observation rendered acute by rational interpretation.*

These remarks about explanatory hypotheses suggest that the role of observation in natural science is not quite so simple as it is sometimes supposed to be. A great and insufficiently recognized part is played by *faith*. If some people had not had faith in certain hypotheses *before* they had been tested, they would never have been tested at all. The attitude of a man of science is not always that of a cautious sceptic but that of a bold explorer with a burning faith that his methods will be successful.

* *Process and Reality* (1929), p. 5.

> Our doubts are traitors
> And make us lose the good we oft might win,
> By fearing to attempt.

These considerations concerning hypotheses suggest the following further reflexions on matters of policy:

(i) Instead of explanatory hypotheses being treated with the *maximum* scepticism when they are *new*, and the *minimum* when they are *old*, a reversal of this policy might be profitable. Thus, in view of the difficulty of inventing them, it is suggested that a welcoming attitude should be adopted towards new explanatory hypotheses and an increasingly critical attitude towards them as they begin to harden into dogmas.

(ii) Every successful hypothesis has the effect of *excluding* something, of shutting up possible channels of investigation, and tends to make people think that our knowledge is far more complete and final than in fact it is. (The discovery of vitamins would not have come as such a surprise as it appears to have done if people had not thought the last word on the physiology of nutrition had been said. See Drummond and Wilbraham, *The Englishman's Food* (1940), p. 320.) The criticism of established hypotheses is therefore necessary to prevent cramping the scope of natural science by limiting investigation to channels that are already familiar. Scepticism regarding established hypotheses should be especially concerned about those directions to which such familiar hypotheses blind us. This is, perhaps, the most important argument in favour of the autonomy of the sciences.

(iii) The occurrence of two or more explanatory hypotheses covering much the same ground—like the corpuscular and the undulatory hypotheses regarding light in physics—is a matter for congratulation rather than one for regret.

(iv) A *merely* rejecting attitude towards a hypothesis is useless because even a bad hypothesis is better than none. A critic should, therefore, have something better to offer in place of the hypothesis he is urging us to abandon. At the same time criticism accompanied by *analysis* of an existing hypothesis may be helpful, if it points out directions in which a new hypothesis may be sought.

(v) It is highly desirable to cultivate a sense of awareness of the type and status of the statements we are using and, when we get into difficulties with explanatory hypotheses, it is always advisable to work back to the observational level from which came the inspiration for their invention, and where their confirmation or refutation is to be sought.

I will conclude this section with a quotation from Professor H. H. Price which clearly has a bearing upon what has been said about explanatory hypotheses and is worth thinking about:

. . . no theory concerning 'microscopical' objects can possibly be used to throw doubt upon our beliefs concerning chairs or cats or rocks, so long as these are based directly on sight and touch. Empirical science can never be more trustworthy than perception upon which it is based; and it can hardly fail to be *less* so, since among its non-perceptual premises there can hardly fail to be some which are neither self-evident nor demonstrable. Thus the not uncommon view that the world which we perceive is an illusion and only the 'scientific' world of protons and electrons is real, is based upon a gross fallacy, and would destroy the very premises upon which science itself depends.*

* *Perception* (1932), p. 1. The 'non-perceptual premises' here referred to are my explanatory hypotheses, or some of them.

§ 7. GETTING

In the preceding sections it has been pointed out that the part played by observation in the building up of explanatory hypotheses is by no means simple and easy to understand. We shall see now that difficulties arise even in connexion with observation records. Even here the relation between a statement and what it is supposed to be about is far from simple. It is very natural to suppose that whenever we talk we talk *about* something, and that we usually know what we are talking about. But when we come to reflect upon the situation we find that it is frequently difficult to say what we are talking about; and in some cases there is reason to believe that although we are talking sense yet we do not know what we are talking about, and we may in fact not be talking about anything at all. There is, for example, no general agreement among experts regarding the question what mathematicians talk about, and the possibility is by no means excluded that they do not talk about anything when they are talking mathematics. (A celebrated palaeontologist once assured me that the subject-matter of mathematics was 'mental processes' because, he said, 'there was nothing else it could be'. It had not occurred to him that this would make mathematics indistinguishable from psychology.) This is a highly paradoxical situation which requires some attention if we are to try to understand what we are doing in natural science.

We can begin to get some insight into these matters by contemplating the following two sentences:

Tom is getting a view of the sea
from his bedroom window (A)

and

Tom is getting a view of the sea in his sleep. (B)

These are sentences of a type which might easily occur in ordinary conversation and we should have no difficulty in understanding them. In the case of (A) we should say that Tom is looking out of the window and seeing the sea; in case (B) we should say that Tom is dreaming of the sea but not seeing the sea at all. Nevertheless, if we cut off the last four words of (A) and the last three of (B) what is left is the same in the two cases. This suggests that the phrase 'view of the sea' is functioning quite differently in the two cases. We have in fact what is called a four-termed relation in (A) and a three-termed one in (B). Consequently 'getting' is also functioning quite differently in the two sentences, and in order to preserve and make clear the difference it will be desirable to write 'getting$_1$' in the first case and 'getting$_2$' in the second. We can make this distinction clear by bracketing the terms in the two sentences thus:

getting$_1$
(Tom) is getting (a view) of (the sea) from (his bedroom window).

getting$_2$
(Tom) is getting (a view of the sea) in (his sleep).

We can also say that in sentence (A) the little word 'of' has a different role from its function in (B). In (A) two objects seem to be involved—a view and the sea—and 'of' seems to be expressing the fact that they stand in a certain relation to one another. In (B) on the other hand there are not two things but only one—the view. In (B) 'of' seems to have a purely classificatory function; it is only telling us what *sort* of view is being got, in the sense of 'sort' in which we should say that a view of Mt Blanc is a view of a different sort from a view of Trafalgar Square, quite independently of the question whether we were seeing Mt Blanc or not. But there is another classification of views of which (B) takes no account, namely a classification into (i) visual memory images, (ii) hallucinatory views, (iii) views got in dreams, and (iv) 'ordinary', non-hallucinatory or veridical views.

The distinction here made between getting$_1$ as a four-termed, and getting$_2$ as a three-termed, relation is helpful in avoiding puzzles that may easily arise in ordinary discourse. For example, when we say that Tom is getting a view of a rainbow from his bedroom window, we seem at first sight to have a case of getting$_1$, but many people would say that it was in fact getting$_2$ because the rainbow is not a term in the relation which is comparable to the sea in our example of getting$_1$. They would say that rainbow and view of rainbow coincide in a way which is impossible in the case of the sea. Similarly, it will be false to say that Tom is getting a view of a bent stick half immersed in water if in fact the stick is straight and we intend getting in the sense of getting$_1$. We can in fact have:

Tom is getting$_1$ a view of a straight stick half immersed in water

and

Tom is getting$_2$ a view of a bent stick half immersed in water,

without contradiction.

Finally, suppose two men (who have heard of but never seen a railway before) are standing facing one another some six yards apart between the rails of a railway line. One, Mr A, says 'These rails are nearer together at your end than at mine.' 'Oh no!' says Mr B, 'they are nearer together at your end than at mine.' 'Are you calling me a liar then?' asks Mr A, beginning to run towards B. 'Yes,' says B, 'if you persist in denying the plainest

evidence of your senses.' 'Very well then, take that,' says
A, 'that is just what I am *not* doing.' With that they come
to blows and become so engrossed in their quarrel that
they do not notice the rapid approach of a train which
knocks them down and cuts them to pieces.

But their ghosts continue the discussion in more
amicable terms. 'Now all is clear,' says the ghost of Mr *A*,
'for now we apprehend as the gods do. I was confusing
getting$_1$ with getting$_2$. What I was getting was distinct
from what you were getting. The views we got were
different, the rails we saw were the same.' 'Yes,' said the
other ghost, 'and I too apprehend something more clearly.
I must forgive you for the entirely unjustified and hasty
attack you made upon me.'

In everyday life, although we are thus occasionally
driven to distinguish between views and the things *of
which* they are views, we nevertheless slip back at other
times into the convenient habit of *not* distinguishing them.
At the same time we usually distinguish between a got
sound and the thing of which it is a sound, between a got
feel and the thing of which it is a feel, between a got smell
and the thing of which it is a smell, and between a got
taste and the thing of which it is a taste. Perhaps we show
this preference for views because they are so much more
diversified than the other sorts of things we get and give
us more scope for making hypotheses about the things of
which they are views; they provide more raw material for
the hypothesis-making powers to work upon. But whether
in fact they are raw material and if so in what sense I make
no assumption here; although doubts may well be thrown
on their rawness by the experience of, as we say, 'mistak-
ing something for something else'. For under such circumstances we first get one view which dissolves and is
replaced by another and more permanent one. First,

perhaps, you get a view of a hedgehog and then this quickly gives way to a view of a fur-lined glove turned inside out. This resembles the process of first trying a hypothesis and then abandoning it for a better one. But it differs from this process in that we do not deliberately seek these hypotheses. We find ourselves already in possession of them when we first begin to reflect about such things. The change also from view of hedgehog to view of glove seems to take place automatically and not as a result of any deliberate action on our part.

Before I continue with my main theme I must give some more examples of getting in order to distinguish still further kinds and in order, if that is possible, to avoid misunderstandings. Consider the following:

> Tom is getting a sound of running water in his
> bathroom.
> Tom is getting a feel of fur by stroking his cat.
> Tom is getting a smell of lavender in his garden.
> Tom is getting a taste of salt by drinking sea-water.

These are all examples of getting$_1$ they are all of the form

( ) is getting ( ) which is of ( ) under circumstance ( ).

Next consider the following:

> Tom is getting angry with Molly.
> Tom is getting a kick out of jazz.
> Tom is getting toothache by eating ice cream.

These I shall call instances of getting$_3$. They are of the form

( ) is getting ( ) under circumstance ( ).

This resembles getting$_2$ in being three-termed, but differs from it in that what is got is not *of* anything beyond the person (Tom) who gets. In this way it differs also from

Tom is getting a prize for physics

which I shall exclude from consideration. All the above examples involve the notion of *receiving*; I shall now give examples of getting which involve the notion of *becoming*.

> Tom is getting drunk on port.
> Tom is getting angry with Molly.
> Tom is getting married tomorrow.

This type of getting will also be excluded from subsequent consideration.*

Our subsequent discussions will be greatly facilitated if we can borrow a little technical terminology from the theory of relations. That is to say, let us call *the things which get* the *first domain of getting* or D_1 for short; I shall also call them persons. Tom in the examples thus belongs to the first domain of getting. The *second domain of getting* will be *the things got*, namely, views, feels, sounds, tastes, etc. This can be called D_2 for short. I propose to include in it not only the second domain of getting$_1$ but also the second domain of getting$_2$ and of getting$_3$. It will thus include *feelings* in a very wide sense of the word. The *third domain of getting* or D_3 will consist of *the things of which* members of D_2 are views or feels or sounds, etc., in the sense of getting$_1$. The fourth domain of getting will consist

---

* It will be noticed that 'Tom is getting angry with Molly' has been given as an example both of getting$_3$ and of getting in the sense of becoming. This has been done deliberately in order to emphasize this source of ambiguity. When we utter this statement we may mean that Tom is getting a certain angry feeling (this would be getting$_3$) or we may mean that Tom is becoming angry. If someone judges that Tom is becoming angry when in fact Tom is not getting a feeling of anger, then we should say that Tom is pretending to be angry.

of circumstances under which getting$_1$ will take place. These are usually described in terms of things belonging to D_3 and do not appear to involve anything new.

The question next to be considered is whether the first three domains of getting are mutually exclusive. It is clear that D_1 and D_2 are mutually exclusive. It would be false or meaningless to say that a view or a sound is getting something or that someone is getting Tom in any of the senses of 'getting' we are taking into consideration. Similarly D_2 and D_3 are mutually exclusive. It would be false or meaningless to say that Tom is getting a view of a view or of a smell or of a sound; and it would be equally false or meaningless to say that Tom is getting the sea of anything. On the other hand D_1 and D_3 are not mutually exclusive. It is quite possible for Tom to get a view of Molly or even of himself (in a mirror). As already stated I am assuming that it will not be necessary to distinguish D_3 from D_4. Not only can Tom get a view of the sea from his bedroom window, he can also get a view of his bedroom window from the sea.

The relations between D_1, D_2 and D_3 can be depicted diagrammatically in the following way:

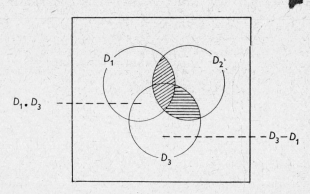

45

The three classes are represented by three circles. The unshaded overlapping area represents the class whose members are common to both D_1 and D_3 and is designated in the diagram by '$D_1 . D_3$'. The three shaded areas are those which, as we have seen, have no members. The three classes with which we shall be concerned in what follows are (i) D_2, (ii) $D_1 . D_3$, and (iii) that part of D_3 which is outside D_1 and is designated in the diagram by $D_3 - D_1$. Little further will be said here about that part of D_1 which is outside D_3.

In talking about these topics it is impossible to avoid some technical terminology and the method here followed provides us with a terminology which is neutral and neither emotionally nor theoretically loaded. To that extent it is superior to the terminologies which have come down to us from the past and are closely associated with the theoretical views of those who have used them. With its help we can now briefly consider some of the traditional attitudes to the above three subdivisions of the domains of getting. These attitudes have usually taken the form of repudiating one or more of the three classes.

First we can consider the view of those who accept D_2 but totally reject D_1 and D_3. This view involves rejecting getting altogether. For if D_1 is empty, then there are no getters. Names used in ordinary language in connexion with D_1 and D_3 must then be regarded as names for complexes of things belonging exclusively to D_2. An upholder of this view cannot say

> Tom is getting a view of a red disk,

he must say

> It reddens circularly.

As a device for solving problems this is the most efficient so far devised because it abolishes all problems. On this view natural science is certainly not occupied with the investigation of a world behind the scenes because there is no such world. The chief objection to this doctrine is the difficulty of believing it without special training, although it has been supported by eminent men of science such as Ernst Mach and Karl Pearson. This difficulty is increased (or perhaps it would be more correct to say created) by the fact that supporters of the doctrine, instead of devising a special language which would have enabled them to speak in a manner consistent with their theory, have continued to use natural language which has developed in relation to a totally different set of beliefs. For that reason upholders of this doctrine frequently expose themselves to the charge of insincerity. Nevertheless the doctrine has some strong points. It must be confessed that there is a sense in which we do not know what we mean by words like 'we' and 'I' and in fact all words which apply to D_1 and D_3. It must also be admitted that there is an element of hypothesis in every statement concerning these two domains of getting. Another strong point of the doctrine under consideration is that the ultimate test of any statement about D_1 or D_3 is by means of getting in one form or another.

Another school of thought rejects D_2. This seems a strange thing to do because it is difficult to understand how anyone can be persuaded to pay good money to enter a picture gallery if there are no views or an orchestral concert if there are no sounds, or indeed what it can mean to say that science is based upon observation. It would be interesting to hear what a defender of this view would say to a proposal that he should undergo a surgical operation without an anaesthetic. For it is clear that if D_2 is empty then anaesthetics are for the benefit of the surgeon, not for the benefit of the patient. And yet this is quite contrary to the ordinary beliefs of patients about anaesthetics.

Some of the people who adopt this theory will agree that seeing is a matter of getting views, but they will put views in D_3; they will interpret the 'of' in the expression 'view of the sea' in the sense of *part of*. They will say that in seeing the sea a part of the surface of the sea is revealed to you. This attitude is confronted with the difficulty of coping with getting$_2$ and with dealing with those situations where common sense recognizes the differences between getting$_1$ and getting$_2$. They must also deal with the problem of explaining why such a specially privileged position should be accorded to views as compared with the other things in D_2. In this context it is particularly important to notice that the distinction between D_2 and D_3 is one which is made in ordinary language and is therefore not the product of a technical vocabulary whether scientific or philosophical. That is clear from our very first examples of getting (A) and (B) on p. 39.

Among other variations on the theme there are those who accept D_1 and D_2 but reject D_3, and again those who accept D_3 and D_2 but reject D_1; but I do not wish to devote space to discussing other types of repudiation of the various domains of getting, because I do not propose to ask the reader to join me in accepting any one of them. In view of the great diversity among men regarding the emptiness or otherwise of the three domains of getting, it would seem that any utterance we may make *must* seem dogmatic from the standpoint of at least one of the various schools of thought. From a detached point of view there would seem to be little to choose between the various possible repudiations. And if that is so why repudiate? Why not admit the possibility that all three domains as well as the area outside (which has not yet been mentioned) are non-empty? This liberal attitude at least has the merit of not exposing us too much to the dangers of missing something. We shall be less liable to the error technically known in philosophy as 'pouring out the baby with the bath water'. We shall be less open to the rebuke which Hamlet cast at the sceptical Horatio, who would not let belief take hold of him. This attitude is further reinforced if we admit the possibility that the various rejections do not so much express empirical findings, or even explanatory hypotheses, as different types of human temperament, or perhaps in the case of repudiation of D_1 and D_2, craft pride and craft prejudice. But the strongest argument in favour of a liberal attitude is this: however much men may differ about the emptiness or otherwise of the various domains of getting, they talk a language which contains words appropriate to all three domains. If therefore we allow the three areas D_1, D_2 and D_3 in our diagram to represent classes of *names*, rather than classes of alleged objects named by those names, we shall at least attain a less dogmatic attitude and one towards which we can hope for much more agreement. For, whatever else it is, physical science is a very successful way of *talking*, which enables us to discover new ways of making and doing things, even although it is very difficult to say, regarding the theoretical or hypothetical part of that talk, what it is all about. However much people may repudiate the ontological beliefs* of individual physicists, the results of their work on the observational level confront us on every hand. We now see that even statements on the observational level involve a hypothesis, according to whether we take the view that they speak about D_3 or D_1 or only about D_2. That is what I had in mind when I said,

---

* By 'ontological beliefs' is here meant beliefs regarding the basic categories of objects in terms of which the world is to be described.

at the beginning of this section, that it seems to be possible to talk sense without being able to say what you are talking about. In what follows I shall talk as though I believed in both divisions of D_3, but I do so in full admission that I thereby adopt a hypothesis, even although it may well be one which cannot be tested.

Nothing has so far been said about what is represented by the area in our diagram which lies outside the three circles and therefore outside the field of getting. This is a very heterogeneous collection. It will include many things, or their names, which belong to sociology, such as societies, cultures, laws, parliaments, clubs, families, etc., all of which presuppose D_1. It will include the abstract entities of pure mathematics such as classes, numbers and relations. Finally, it will include things which are mentioned in natural science but which do not have views, sounds, feels, smells, etc., which are *of* them. Thus not everything is covered by the notion of the domains of getting.

§ 8. DOING

IF we repudiate D_1 and D_3 there can be no distinction between doing and getting, no genuine difference between, say, getting a view of a cow and milking a cow. Our life must be passed entirely in getting; as though we were embedded in concrete, except that of course if there were no D_3 there would be no concrete, and if there were no D_1 there would be no 'we'. Perhaps this is a rather unfair way of expressing the situation, but at all events if D_3 is rejected, all doing must be 'reduced' (as it is called) to getting of various kinds. If, however, we are allowed D_3

then we can not only have doing as something distinct from getting, but doing can come to the aid of getting. For, apart from doing how are we to distinguish veridical getting (getting$_1$) from other kinds of getting? If Tom wants to convince himself that the view he is getting of the sea is not hallucinatory, one way in which he can proceed is by taking a walk and taking a bathe in the sea. But from the standpoint of the persistent rejecter of D_3 this argument will carry no conviction. He will say that all this doing can be translated into getting, but the process of translating will present great difficulties on account of the paucity of the vocabulary of getting. The rejecter of D_3 will be compelled to invent a hypothesis to explain this lack of vocabulary. It is strange that we should have such a linguistic abundance for talking about things which do not exist and such poverty for talking about things which do. Nevertheless let us concede our opponent his hypothesis and, while differing from him, let us admit that in adopting D_3 we also are adopting a hypothesis and not claiming to be in exclusive possession of the truth.

When once we are allowed doing as an activity distinct from getting this will perhaps be the place in which to mention a possible difference there may be between doing as it is treated in the psychological and social sciences on the one hand, and doing as it is dealt with in the physical sciences on the other. In the first case we deal with acts of persons and are interested in such questions as motivation and aim, and whether acts are intentional, accidental or compulsory, etc. We abstract from the fact that the realization of aims by doing involves muscles, nerves, etc. But when doing is viewed from the standpoint of the physical sciences then just the opposite happens. We are then interested in doing as something involving muscles and nerves and we abstract from motivation and other psychological aspects. If the results of the two methods appear to conflict, it is usually forgotten that they both involve abstraction and instead recourse is had to explaining away. We can perhaps express the distinction by saying that in the first case we are interested in doing as acts of members of D_1 and in the second case we are concerned with it wholly within $D_3 - D_1$. What is required is a method of dealing with the possible peculiarities of things belonging to $D_1 . D_3$.

In discussions of aims or purposes the notion of *end* is frequently employed in two *quite different senses*. First, it may be that what is intended is something appropriate to D_1 as we have suggested above, some wish, hope, aim or intention. The second meaning is of the terminus of some process in $D_3 - D_1$. An example of the first would be a persistent desire of some person to possess a home of his own; the corresponding example of the second meaning would be the completion of an actual physical house in which to live—the laying of the last brick, or the spreading of the last piece of wall-paper or carpet—so that the lucky possessor can at last say: Now my hopes have been realized!

Now in a psychological law we should have, among the causal factors involved in the building of the house, the ends of the future owner in the *first* sense of 'end', but clearly not in the second sense. These two uses of 'end' can I think be discerned in the following passage:

When an organism is motivated only by instinct and environment, we call the result its *behaviour*; when, on the other hand, the organism is not only influenced by these hereditary and environmental forces, but by a conscious ideal or end towards which it is directed, we call it *conduct*, for our actions conduce or lead to that end. So we speak of the 'behaviour' of animals, but the 'conduct' of men. Moreover, the 'end' assumes a different character. Every instinctive action leads to some result or *end*, but when that end is consciously conceived and voluntarily pursued, we call it a *purpose*. So we speak of the 'ends' of nature, for nature is innocent of any conscious aim, but of the 'purposes' of man.*

§ 9. TALKING

IT is difficult to exaggerate the all-pervading importance of talk. The difficulty is rather the other way: we take talk so much for granted that it is difficult to appreciate fully the many roles it plays in our life. Talking, like doing, is a supplement to getting. If Tom does not want to take a walk or a bathe he can ask a passer-by whether he too is getting a view of the sea, and by such means he can satisfy himself that his own view of the sea is veridical and not hallucinatory. It is thus by talking as well as by doing that we achieve objectivity, and getting becomes, in a sense, not purely personal but interpersonal. If doing and the belief which accompanies successful doing is the gateway (metaphorically speaking) to D_3, so we can say that talking, accompanied by the feeling of sympathy, is the gateway to D_1, the 'way into a man's heart', as we say in the time-honoured metaphor.

Both physics and psychology involve talking and faith in the assumption that persons are not *all* habitual liars. Talk thus enters into all medical diagnosis and treatment, except when the patient is unconscious (and so is not getting anything) and it is by means of talking that we

* J. A. Hadfield, *Psychology and Morals* (1927), p. 84.

'give ourselves away' by revealing our beliefs, prejudices and crimes.

Getting, doing and talking thus form an intertwined triad which, when its elements are taken together, enables us to make sense of the contribution of each, in a way which is impossible when the constituents are considered separately. Moreover, it is persons who get and do and talk. They seem thus to be inseparably involved in D_1.

So far I have spoken as though talking was only important from the point of view of the cognitive processes, but its share in other aspects of our life is not less immense. We appreciate this when we recall its importance as a medium of certain of the arts and its part in religious and social activities. Particularly relevant here is its role both as a pathogenic and a therapeutic agent. It is a widely held hypothesis in psychopathology that wounds inflicted by talk in early life may contribute later to the development of neurosis. The time is not far distant when it was considered incompatible with a man's honour not to avenge with physical weapons wounds inflicted by talk. Even in some hospitals at the present day talk as a source of wounds is recognized as much as an enemy of health as staphylococci and other more orthodox pathogenic agents. This is clear from the remarks of Dr Richard Asher in the lecture on the seven sins of medicine which was mentioned in §1. He says:

Mental cruelty is common and arises in three ways: (1) by saying too much; (2) by saying too little; and (3) by the patient being forgotten. By saying too much we often burden a patient with a load of anxiety which adds to the illness we are trying to relieve. . . . Before telling a patient anything of his illness it is essential to consider whether it will help him or harm him. . . .

By saying too little one can cause the fear of the unknown;

the gaps may be filled in by the patient with alarming inventions and superstitions . . . in these cases reassurance is more important than medicine, and it is the doctor's duty to dig out these fears if possible.

Lastly, forgetting the patient. I refer to that kind of bedside teaching and discussion where the patient is treated as if he were unconscious, or discussed as if he already lay on the necropsy slab. It must be remembered that patients have ears, and that *sotto voce* murmurings about polysyllabic diseases strike needless terror into their hearts.*

That such warnings should be felt to be necessary is perhaps an indication of the degree to which the physical sciences predominate in the teaching of medical students.

The value of talk as a therapeutic agent was understood in former times: 'Give sorrow words; the grief that does not speak Whispers the o'erfraught heart, and bids it break.' In modern times it has been repeatedly recognized and Freud provided an explanatory hypothesis concerning its mode of action. By reference to the part played by talk in their recovery we can divide sick persons into five classes:

(1) Sick persons who can be restored to health by the ordinary methods of medicine and surgery without the deliberate use of talk as a therapeutic agent.

(2) Sick persons who can be restored to health by the ordinary methods of medicine and surgery *only* when these are supplemented by talk which arouses only ordinary memories and is used deliberately and systematically as a therapeutic agent.

(3) Sick persons who are diagnosed as belonging to (1) but who can in fact be restored to health by talk which

* *The Lancet*, 27 August 1949, p. 359. See also the article entitled 'Psychology and the maternity unit', by Elizabeth Tylden, *The Lancet*, 2 February 1952, p. 231.

arouses only ordinary memories and is used deliberately and systematically as a therapeutic agent but *without* the help of ordinary methods of medicine and surgery.

(4) Sick persons who can be restored to health neither by the ordinary methods of medicine and surgery, nor by talk, which arouses only ordinary memories, deliberately and systematically used as a therapeutic agent, but are restored to health either by some special physical method such as electric convulsion therapy, or by some special technique involving talk which arouses memories which are not otherwise accessible, e.g. by hypnosis or psycho-analysis.

(5) Sick persons who cannot be restored to health by any known method.

Examples of classes (1), (4) and (5) need not be given. But I will give what can I think be regarded for the present, tentatively at least, as examples of classes (2) and (3). The example of (2) is from an article by Dr George Day in *The Lancet*, 11 October 1952, p. 694:

A young girl, an economics student at a provincial university, developed tuberculosis. She came from an academically brilliant family; father one of the important backroom advisers of the country; elder brother and sister both easy double firsts. The cause of the young girl's breakdown was alleged to be overwork. It was quite true: she had been overworking. But with complete rest, pneumothorax treatment, and antibiotics she did not make the expected progress. Weeks and months went by. She seemed eager to get back to the university, but her return did not seem to get any nearer. Then she divulged that she had found it excessively difficult to keep up with those whom she regarded as her peers. So she was subjected to a battery of intelligence tests, and they showed what she had suspected but had always refused to face. She had not a first-class intelligence; she was a safe second class, but she had not got the equipment to compete with the rest of the family. This came as a great relief, and her recovery dated from this re-orientation. On discharge she took up shorthand and typing, and was gold medallist for her year. She then got a good responsible job in a municipal office. In her spare time she amuses herself with free-lance journalism. Her original goal was impossible of attainment—and her spirit failed her.

My example of class (3) is from Curran and Guttman's *Psychological Medicine* (1945). They describe the case of a girl who developed an abdominal pain and consulted a surgeon. He recommended an operation for the removal of the appendix and this was accordingly performed. But after recovery and convalescence the girl again complained of abdominal pain. This time she was advised to consult a surgeon with a view to treatment for adhesions resulting from the first operation. But the second surgeon referred the girl to a psychiatrist from whose inquiries it transpired that the girl's education had been such that she believed it to be possible to become pregnant by being kissed. The first abdominal pain had appeared after the experience of being kissed by an undergraduate during his vacation. After the recovery from the operation this girl was again kissed by the same undergraduate with a similar result. When the relevant facts about human reproduction had been explained to her the girl had no further trouble and when last heard of she was rowing in a women's eight.

It seems clear that illnesses of class (1) are those commonly referred to as physical; those of class (4) are the so-called mental, and those of classes (2) and (3) are the psychosomatic diseases. Many more examples of (2) and (3) will be found in the book *Mind and Body : Psychosomatic Medicine* (1947), by Dr Flanders Dunbar.

§ 10. SCIENCE AND METAPHYSICS

Sooner or later in discussions of the present kind the word 'metaphysics' appears. It is not infrequently used as a term of abuse. A considerable part is played in exchanges of opinion of all kinds by the application to other peoples' beliefs of polite but opprobrious epithets of which 'metaphysics' is one. If you do not like some particular doctrine, and you are unkind enough to wish to embarrass the person who is defending it, it suffices to declare with emphasis that it is metaphysical. This has the double advantage of being obscure and denigratory. It is obscure because it is difficult to say what it means and for that reason the charge is difficult to rebut. It is denigratory because it is widely believed that, in some obscure way, metaphysics is disreputable. Now because metaphysics is held to be disreputable, efforts have been made from time to time to distinguish metaphysical statements from scientific ones. At one time it was thought that the distinction could be based on the supposed fact that scientific statements could be verified and metaphysical ones could not. Unfortunately this view had to be abandoned when it was seen that scientific generalizations and explanatory hypotheses could not be verified in the sense of being known to be true. Then it was thought that, while scientific explanatory hypotheses could not be verified, because the observations that would be required to verify them could not possibly be made, yet they could be falsified, because a single negative instance suffices to negate a universal general statement. It is alleged that metaphysical statements make, so to speak, no contact with observation at all, not even through their consequences, and so cannot be falsified. Unfortunately the situation is not quite so simple as this view would suggest. It is not always easy to decide whether a statement is falsifiable or not. Attention has already been drawn to the important part played in science, at least as far as explanatory hypotheses are concerned, by the will to believe and the process of explaining away. As we have seen, when an explanatory hypothesis has been in use for some time and has proved its worth, both as a means of bringing together a host of lesser generalizations, and as a fruitful promoter of research, it becomes for many a kind of vested interest. People dislike chopping and changing. Many will therefore resist any assault on a cherished hypothesis and will seize upon any device which suggests itself as a means of defence, and will use all the resources at their disposal to explain away observation records or other objections which threaten their favourite hypothesis. It is easy to find examples of this. Consider, for example, the doctrine that every person seeks the maximum of pleasure. At first sight this seems to be refuted by the occurrence of martyrs who sacrifice their lives for some moral or religious principle. But the *status quo* is easily restored for anyone who wishes to restore it by the hypothesis that in such cases the victims believe that they will be compensated for the loss of earthly pleasures by the far greater pleasures of heavenly bliss. Again it has been urged against the doctrine of evolutionary change by natural selection that the development of organs like the wings of birds, which would be useless while they were too small for flight, would be impossible by such a method. As mere rudimentary wings they would be useless. Such objections can always be met by the hypothesis* that the

* It is important to notice (and this is sometimes forgotten) that the mere fact that someone can think of a hypothesis for explaining away achieves nothing unless some additional data are at the same time brought forward in support of it.

development of such organs was linked genetically with the formation of some other feature which was of such high survival value as to compensate for the lack of it in the wings. So long as such supplementary hypothesis-making is allowed, such doctrines cannot be refuted. The use of explaining away thus very much complicates the business of falsifying explanatory hypotheses and diminishes the value of falsifiability as a criterion for distinguishing them from metaphysical statements. The criterion might also be assailed from the other side. It is possible to point to the fact that, however it may have come about, in the course of time metaphysical doctrines have flourished and have later fallen out of favour.

Nevertheless, whether we accept falsifiability as a satisfactory and sharp criterion for distinguishing scientific from metaphysical statements or not, it does draw attention to a point which should be kept in mind. For it is clear that an explanatory hypothesis which is easily bolstered up by recourse to explaining away might easily have a serious retarding effect on the branch of science to which it belongs. Any attempt to break away and explore fresh territory would be too easily met by new barriers erected in favour of the *status quo*.

It could also be argued that in the past metaphysical doctrines have been of some service to science. Even theology has been a source of bright ideas, as A. N. Whitehead has pointed out in connexion with Maupertuis's discovery of the principle of least action.*

It might be said that scientific statements only claim to have application on the observational level to the things of everyday life; whereas metaphysical statements claim to tell us about a world (called Reality) behind the scenes of everyday life (called Appearance). This distinction

* See his *Science and the Modern World* (1927), p. 77.

between appearance and reality is not confined to metaphysics but is part of the technique of explaining away. One of the commonest devices of controversy is to dismiss anything you do not like as 'mere appearance'. What we want to believe we call reality and what we do not want to believe we call appearance. In daily life the distinction between reality and appearance usually occurs between the things of D_2 which are, and the things of D_2 which are not, *of* something in D_3. But in some metaphysical and all physical theories the whole of D_2 is classified as appearance and only D_3 is permitted to claim the title of reality. It is difficult to see therefore how a clear distinction can be drawn between science and metaphysics along these lines, especially when the difficulties explained in §7 are remembered.

The notion of reality is connected with another obscure notion which plays a large part in metaphysical discussions, namely the notion of existence. Existence is thought of as something absolute and yet what can it mean out of relation to getting, doing and talking? In the case of something like toothache existing and being got by someone seem to coincide. People believe in horses because they can get views, feels, smells, etc., of them and because they can ride them and do other things with them; and similarly with other things belonging to D_3. Finally people believe in electrons and such things because talk about them is helpful and can guide them in doing things in laboratories and workshops. This relativity of 'existence' is illustrated by the history of science. In the days of Maxwell and Hertz physicists found that affirmative talk involving aether waves was helpful, and at that time an aether was said to exist. Then came Einstein who found that he could do without an aether, which accordingly was no longer said to exist. Recently, however, a letter appeared in *Nature* under the title: 'Is there an Aether?' by Professor P. A. M. Dirac. This letter did not announce that its author had succeeded in getting a view or a feel or a sound of an aether; it related how he had hit upon a way of formulating certain physical laws which involved affirmative talk of an aether. It looks very much therefore as though, when we find it helpful to use a notion in scientific talk, we tend to believe in the existence of something which is said to correspond to that notion. Then, if and when this kind of talk ceases to be helpful, we cease to say that the thing talked about exists. At the same time this practice seems to be combined with a doctrine which is rather difficult to reconcile with it. The aether, if it exists, is supposed to do so without our help and irrespective of whether we get views of it or talk affirmatively about it or not. It is not supposed that it can be called into or dismissed from existence by a stroke of a mathematician's pen. And yet we cannot possibly know whether it exists in such a sense because we do not know what changes of opinion may occur among mathematical physicists in the future. It can exist *for us* without there being any guarantee that it will exist *for them*. This suggests that it is difficult to distinguish *existing* from *existing for* someone.

Considerations of the above kind seem to cast doubts on the utility and importance of the notion of existence. One reason for doubting its importance is that it seems to be impossible to know that something exists without knowing something else about it. On the other hand, if you do know something more about it, then you do not need to be told that it exists. In a text-book of astronomy, alongside the statement that the moon is the only satellite of the earth, no one would expect to find the additional statement that the moon exists. On the other hand there are times when it is difficult to express what we want to express without using the notion of existence. For example, how are we to describe the distinction between

Columbus discovered America

and

Columbus created America

except by saying that we accept the first of these statements because we believe that America existed before Columbus arrived there?

From the notion of existence we turn now to criteria for applying it. One very common criterion is that which requires views to be confirmed by tactual feels, as in the celebrated soliloquy of Macbeth about whether he was getting a view of a dagger in the sense of getting$_1$ or of getting$_2$. This criterion gives rise to a metaphysical theory which we can call the finger and thumb philosophy. Its object is what is called the billiard-ball universe. According to this doctrine a thing exists if it can *in principle* be picked up in the finger and thumb. Macbeth's dagger failed to satisfy this requirement. The reservation 'in principle' is necessary in order not to exclude such things as planets and atoms which are billiard balls on too large or too small a scale for human picking up. (The criterion is thus abandoned when it is inconvenient.)

Another tenet of this philosophy seems to be that everything that is is in a big box called space which is floating down a river called time. Consequently if anything (except the river!) is not in space it just is not at all. That is why D_2 is unpopular in some circles.* You cannot pick up a view or a smell or a sound or a feel or a taste between your

* A. N. Whitehead has discussed this view of spatial relations under the title of *simple location*. See his *Science and the Modern World* (1927), pp. 61, 72, 89, 114 and 128.

finger and thumb. Through a combination of getting, doing and talking we build up useful ways of talking about spatial relations, but these are relations of which the terms all belong to D_3. If I want to know whether the thing of which I am getting a view is a matchbox containing matches I first *do* something to it. I pick it up and shake it. If I then get a certain characteristic sound I say to myself: Ah! that sounds hopeful! Then I do something else, I open the box. If I now get a view of a match in a certain characteristic relation to a view of a box my hopes are confirmed, and my investigation is concluded if I can pick out a match and light it. When I take out a match I may get a view of my hand picking out a match, but what I pick out is not the view of the match but the match itself. Getting is an affair of D_2; doing of D_3. The view of the match is not inside the box in the sense in which the match is inside the box. Neither is it inside the head of the getter in the sense in which the match is inside the box, although this belief seems to be widely held. For if you open a person's skull you do not expect to get, still less to see, the views he is getting. You cannot see a view; you can only get it. It seems then that for anyone who accepts D_2 (and thus prefers to have his surgical operations under an anaesthetic) the box theory of space and the finger and thumb philosophy will not suffice. The world is not so simple as these theories represent it. In addition to things which have spatial relations with one another (the things of D_3) we have to recognize another mode of relation between things. To express this difference I shall say that the things of D_2 are *atopically* related to those of D_3. Thus Tom's toothache is atopically related to the ice cream. No one need be shocked at this. It is only shocking if we take the billiard-ball universe too dogmatically. But as physics has long ago abandoned the billiard-ball universe as a dogma we are in good company if we do not take it dogmatically.

Another metaphysical doctrine which should be briefly mentioned is that of substance and attribute. This is connected with the linguistic pair: subject and predicate. A great many sentences in natural language have the same form as

Tom is clever

in which the word 'Tom' is said to be the subject and the phrase 'is clever' the predicate. According to the metaphysical doctrine in question such a sentence is said to ascribe the *attribute* of cleverness to Tom who is called a *substance*. Thus the world consists of things or substances which are the supporters or coat-hangers for a clothing (metaphorically speaking) of attributes, qualities or properties. This doctrine does not appear to tell us very much, and does not deserve to be taken so seriously as to constitute a dogmatic barrier to the invention of explanatory hypotheses which may not seem to be in agreement with it. Neither need we regard the subject-predicate type of sentence as something ultimate and inevitable. We are free, if we wish, to construct languages for scientific purposes which do not involve a distinction between subject and predicate.*

This brief reference to the substance-attribute metaphysics will serve to illustrate a point which helps to distinguish metaphysical from scientific statements. The former are always very general, they also claim to be very comprehensive but at the same time they do not condescend to go into details. Natural science, as we have seen, always works in the opposite direction—from the

* For an example see my paper 'Science without properties' in the *British Journal for the Philosophy of Science*, vol. II (1951), pp. 193–216.

particular to the increasingly general. Whitehead's 'habitual working gauge of science' has already been quoted, namely the question 'Has the doctrine a precise application to a variety of particular circumstances, so as to determine the exact phenomena which should be observed?' It is this application to a variety of particular circumstances so as to determine the exact phenomena which should be observed which we miss in metaphysical theories. There is obviously an affinity here between this working gauge and the requirements of falsifiability. In another place Whitehead has written: 'Too large a generalization leads to mere barrenness. It is the large generalization, limited by a happy particularity, which is the fruitful conception.'*

It is for reasons of these kinds that the discussions which are always going on about the relation between body and mind do not seem to me to be very helpful to medical psychology. It is difficult to see how anything that could be called a solution of this alleged problem can come out of extremely general considerations. If we want a general hypothesis which will embrace both the physical and the mental aspects of our life, we must be patient and wait until we can reach it by the method of science, i.e. starting from particular observations, passing to generalizations of these, and from this level to increasingly general explanatory hypotheses. It seems pretty plain that not very much progress has yet been made along these lines.

Another example of metaphysical disputation is furnished by the controversies about whether human beings are machines or not, upon which acres of paper and gallons of ink have been expended. Less effort would have been needed if the disputants had distinguished between

* *Science and the Modern World* (1927), p. 39.

being machine-like and being a machine. To be machine-like is to resemble machines in at *least one* respect; and everyone can satisfy himself that he is machine-like by experimenting with his knee-jerk. What makes this controversy metaphysical is the fact that the disputants are not content with this. They require that men should *be* machines and thus resemble machines in *every* essential respect.

It is easy to show that no machine can resemble the man who made it in every respect. For suppose a man, Mr A, makes a machine M. Then M differs from Mr A in at least one respect because Mr A has made a machine and M has not. Even if we allow M to make a machine N, this will not overcome the difficulty because now, although M has made a machine, Mr A has made a machine which has made a machine and so is still one up on M. And so on, however many times you repeat the process, so long as it is finite, Mr A will be one up on M.

But perhaps it will be objected that this is not an essential respect in which they differ. One essential feature of machines is that they are invented and made by a person to perform some task *better than* that person could perform it unaided. Thus a lever helps us to lift heavy weights which we could not otherwise move. A printing machine enables us to duplicate books at a greater rate than is possible by hand, and so on. This is an essential respect because no one would give himself the trouble and expense of inventing and making a contraption which performed some task *less well* than he could perform it with his unaided hands. If therefore men resemble machines in every essential respect, then they must be made by some person or persons to perform some task better than those persons can perform it without their aid. To uphold their theory the supporters of this doctrine must therefore produce such a person. Who can it be? Clearly not the God of Christian theology. Because the God of Christian theology is by a uniformly acknowledged postulate the most perfect being, and if this is so making a machine to perform some task better than he can perform it himself is clearly incompatible with his perfection. If men are machines they must have been made by persons inferior to themselves. In view of these difficulties it would seem that those who wish to emphasize the machine-like features of men would be well advised to content themselves with saying that men are machine-like, rather than that they are machines. Then there will be nothing to dispute about and time and effort can be spent more profitably.

In conclusion let me say that what appears to me to be important in the present context is not so much whether we are to label a statement as scientific or metaphysical but whether we take an attitude towards it which is dogmatic in a bad sense. We cannot always sit on the fence in a state of perpetual scepticism; sooner or later we have to make up our minds and take up a dogmatic attitude. But we can distinguish two kinds of dogmatism. One kind freely acknowledges its dogmatic nature. It says: 'I am taking up this position because in the present state of knowledge it seems to me to be one which will lead to a result which I believe to be desirable.' The other kind of dogmatism says: 'The world is how I say it is. This has been proved by science and may now be regarded as settled for all time. So let us have no more of this nonsense about explanatory hypotheses. We are dealing with unalterable fact.' This is an example of what I mean by dogmatism in the bad sense. It is bad because it may have the effect of bolting and barring doors which may lead to new discoveries.

§ 11. SCIENCE AND ABSTRACTION

It is well recognized that each science is characterized by a particular mode of abstraction, that is to say of concentrating on certain aspects of things and ignoring others. Thus physics abstracts from chemical composition as well as from D_1 and D_2. Chemistry abstracts from geological history and biological involvement. The biological sciences, like all the physical sciences, abstract from psychological and sociological considerations. With physics in mind, A. N. Whitehead wrote:

Its methodological procedure is exclusive and intolerant, and rightly so. It fixes attention on a definite group of abstractions, neglects everything else, and elicits every scrap of information and theory which is relevant to what it has retained. This method is triumphant, provided that the abstractions are judicious. But, however triumphant, the triumph is within limits.*

Although this is clear and well known it seems curiously enough to be forgotten when people begin to philosophize or to consider the mutual relations between the sciences. In spite of the fact that the physical sciences deal only with $D_3 - D_1$ it is frequently claimed that they suffice— or will some day suffice—to cope even with those aspects of things from which abstraction was made. Instead of each science being encouraged to go its own way, to develop in the directions and with the methods which its own exponents think fit, as chemistry and physics originally did, having no precedents or models to follow, some sciences are held to be subordinate to others. In this way it is thought that psychology must be subservient to neurology, some even going so far as to believe that

* *Science and the Modern World* (1927), p. 249.

psychology as such is unnecessary, its whole place being destined to be taken by neurology.

Now it is open to the experts in any science to say 'we propose to abstract from such and such features of what we are studying'; but it is not necessary to say 'all other sciences must follow our example or be condemned as "unscientific" '. Neither is it necessary to believe that what is abstracted from 'does not exist' or 'is an illusion of common sense'. But this is just what happens when we turn physics into the finger and thumb philosophy and in the process throw overboard everything from which physics abstracts. This is a typical example of explaining away in order dogmatically to uphold a particular hypothesis. It is this finger and thumb philosophy which leads medical men to seek a sick *organ* in each sick person, and to label him as 'functional' if such a sick organ is not to be found. It is this same finger and thumb philosophy which demands that everything not belonging to $D_3 - D_1$ must have what is called a *physical basis* therein. This is one way of dealing with what I have called atopical relations: it concentrates attention on the D_3 end of the relation. This finger and thumb philosophy has worked well in certain domains otherwise it would have been abandoned long ago; but remember the 211,000 beds occupied by mental patients mentioned on p. 2!

Among the things from which the physical sciences abstract is the notion of activity. This primarily belongs to persons and thus belongs to D_1. There is no activity in the billiard-ball universe. All that happens is that the balls push or pull one another; but one pushes another only when it has itself been pushed or pulled.

Then there is the notion of purpose. This is rightly excluded from the considerations of physics or must be explained away by it. It is therefore excluded from the billiard-ball universe. But persons talk as though they entertained purposes or had aims and intentions which they try from time to time to realize in the world. Indeed, the explanatory hypotheses of physics are hypotheses which persons have *invented* for the *purpose* of finding their way about in the world of doing; for the *purpose* of realizing their wishes, or satisfying their curiosity and promoting their self-esteem. All this seems plain on the observational level. And yet clusters of billiard balls do not have wishes or invent hypotheses as far as we know. If therefore we wish to adhere dogmatically to the finger and thumb philosophy with its billiard-ball universe, we must devise ways of explaining away all this talk of purpose and intentions. With sufficient ingenuity this can doubtless be done. But let it not be done at the expense of another alternative, namely to recognize the abstractness of physics, to refuse to turn it into the finger and thumb philosophy and to study the worlds of D_1 and D_2 without bias, letting them dictate to us the appropriate bright ideas and apparatus for expressing them. It will then make sense to talk about the purpose of a scientific experiment.

Again, the law and the churches recognize a distinction between 'doing something because you could not help it' and 'doing something deliberately' on which legal and moral responsibility are based. But in the billiard-ball universe there is no such distinction. When one billiard ball bumps up against another it is always because it could not help it. But if we reject the billiard-ball universe or the finger and thumb philosophy of which it is the expression, we can study this distinction with reference to persons and it will make sense to talk about choosing between one scientific hypothesis and another.

Finally we are told that we must not be anthropomorphic in the physical sciences because what applies to persons does not apply to the things studied in physics. (It is thus tacitly admitted that anthropomorphic ideas do apply to persons.) But then when we leave physics and turn to persons we are told that we must only study them by the methods and bright ideas of physics and therefore we must not be anthropomorphic!

It is in such a setting—the finger and thumb philosophy with its billiard-ball universe—that psychology has struggled to develop. It is open to anyone to accept the billiard-ball universe if he wishes to do so; with a liberal use of explaining away it will suffice for many medical purposes. But I do wish to suggest that anyone who chooses to adhere to this point of view might take a charitable and not a dogmatic attitude towards the work of his psychological colleague, who is struggling with the very difficult task of finding a system of hypotheses which will cover the ground from which the physical sciences abstract.

§ 12. RECAPITULATION

IT is now high time to pause for a moment to run over the outlines of our argument lest we lose sight for too long of the wood amidst the abundance of trees.

We began by contrasting the very small part played by psychology in the training of doctors with the very considerable part played by mental illness in contemporary life. It was suggested that the lopsidedness of the medical curriculum (in this country) in this respect might very largely be the result of the enormous success and consequent prestige of the physical sciences, which has led people to identify science with the physical sciences and so to neglect other kinds of investigation. It was also pointed out that this enormous success of the physical sciences was—at least as far as medical students are concerned—accompanied by no attempt at a critical evaluation of scientific statements. This led to §§ 4, 5 and 6 in which natural science was represented as consisting of systems of statements ordered by the consequence relation. We saw how necessary it is to distinguish at least three kinds of scientific statement: (i) observation records, (ii) generalizations of observation records, and (iii) explanatory hypotheses. It is important to distinguish these because much that is true of one kind is not true of the others. We saw the important part played by faith in reaching these statements in addition to the part played by observation. Even observation records involve a complicated interplay of getting, doing and talking. But it is in regard to explanatory hypotheses that there is most scope for misunderstanding and misuse. We saw that there is no way of knowing when an explanatory hypothesis is true, and even when one is contradicted by observation records it is often possible to continue to maintain a hypothesis by the process of explaining away. Such hypotheses are thus pre-eminently statements regarding which it is possible to be dogmatic in a harmful way. Because each hypothesis excludes other hypotheses which, if they could be brought forward and worked out, might lead to new discoveries.

The reader will have guessed that these considerations have been urged upon him with the object of thawing out some of the dogmas to which he may have been brought up and about which he may not previously have thought very deeply. If he is not much interested in medical psychology, it is hoped that at least these considerations may help him to take a tolerant attitude towards it. If he is interested in medical psychology, it is hoped that what has been pointed out may offer him some encouragement and possibly some help in seeking new directions and methods for psychology which are alternative to the particular line of development which the physical sciences have taken in the course of history and which have been in part conditioned by the particular explanatory hypotheses they have adopted.

§ 13. THE CRITICS OF PSYCHOLOGY

THE considerations of §6 led to the drawing-up of certain tentative methodological rules. The first of these rules suggested that instead of explanatory hypotheses being treated with the *maximum* scepticism when they are *new*, and the *minimum* when they are *old*, a reversal of this policy might be profitable; especially in view of the scarcity of fruitful explanatory hypotheses. I propose to give an example of the customary procedure, which is relevant to our present problem. It is to be found in the chapter entitled 'What is wrong with Psychoanalysis?' in the book *Uses and Abuses of Psychology* (1953) by Dr H. J. Eysenck. His discussion is largely bound up with the distinction, made by some German philosophers, between *verstehende* (verstehen = to understand) and *erklärende* (erklären = to explain) psychology. It is plain from what the author himself says that *verstehende* psychology corresponds approximately to what I have been calling observation—or zero-level psychology, and *erklärende* psychology to psychology which includes explanatory hypotheses, e.g. the explanatory hypotheses of Freud concerning repression and the unconscious. From what I have said it will I hope be clear that there is no intention on my part to advocate rejecting the former in favour of the latter. Neither does the former cease to be useful because we have succeeded in passing to theoretical levels. On the contrary, every explanatory hypothesis in psychology, as well as in every other science, can be tested only by confronting it with statements belonging to the observational level which follow from it, including statements belonging to homely everyday person language. But Dr Eysenck asserts that *verstehende* psychology is 'essentially non-scientific and to be judged in terms of belief and faith, rather than in terms of proof and verification'. But this is to reveal a complete misunderstanding of empirical science. I hope earlier sections have made it abundantly clear that all empirical science (i.e. natural science as contrasted with mathematics) rests on belief and faith and not on observation alone; that there can be no final verification of scientific hypotheses in the literal sense of the word 'verification'; and that when such a hypothesis is said to be proved all that is meant is, not that it has been proved in the mathematical sense, but that it has been tested and that so far no observation which contradicts it has yet been made, or at least none that cannot be explained away. It does *not* mean that no such observation will *ever* be made because no one knows or can know such a thing.

Dr Eysenck now proceeds to assert (as he himself says 'briefly and dogmatically') that psychoanalysis is *verstehende* rather than *erklärende* psychology and therefore (according to him) 'essentially non-scientific'. But this can only be said if you insist upon identifying science with physical science, or at least if you recognize no scientific method which does not closely follow the model commonly supposed to be furnished by physics. Dr Eysenck insists on thinking of science (so it seems to me) in a purely static way which makes no provision for future developments (cf. my second policy maxim on p. 37). He says 'The claim that psychoanalysis is scientific has no ascertainable meaning whatever unless we define the term "science" in the way agreed on by the great majority of those who have considered the history and practice of science.' But this is clearly to take an authoritarian and legalistic attitude (looking to the past rather than to the future) towards questions of meaning which says, in effect, 'there is something called "meaning of the word 'science'"" which has been fixed once and for all by a body of experts; anyone who deviates from this by one iota is mistaken and must be branded with the terrible word "unscientific"'. Psychoanalysts belong, according to Dr Eysenck, in such company as Mrs Baker Eddy, Communists, Marxists and the palmist on Brighton pier (a strange collection!).

Disputes of this kind seem to be futile because they depend on differences of *attitude*. Dr Eysenck takes what seems to me to be a static attitude towards the question 'how shall we use the word "science"?' I prefer the view that as new sciences and new methods arise and develop so we must be prepared for revisions in our notions about what is to be called scientific.

The whole argument is in any case a *non sequitur* because it is not the case that psychoanalysis contains no explanatory hypotheses and is therefore *verstehende* psychology. It contains in fact plenty of explanatory hypotheses which we owe to the bright ideas of Sigmund Freud and some of which at least can be tested by clinical observation in the consulting room. But Dr Eysenck will have none of this. He asks 'What then is the evidence on which psychoanalysis is based?' He answers 'Essentially it is clinical rather than experimental'. But that is no reason

for condemning psychoanalysis. Some important discoveries have been made in medicine with purely clinical
methods without the help of experiment.* Undoubtedly
it is a great help to have experimental data, but even
astronomy manages to get along without them; at least
no one has performed experiments with planets and stars.
It would be pedantic in the extreme to reject all procedures which do not have a fool-proof experimental basis
and it would be a great misfortune if all clinical observation were to be despised and condemned as unscientific.
Freud based his more important hypotheses on his
experience with patients; it is difficult to see how otherwise he could have proceeded with his task. In so far as
his hypotheses are founded on clinical experience it is
chiefly by clinical experience that they can be tested. It
must be fully admitted that there are special difficulties
about testing psychological statements of this kind, not
only because they are psychological, but also on account
of the personal and confidential character of the doctor-
patient relationship. If psychoanalysis is not science, there
seems to be no point in applying to it methods and criteria
of criticism which are appropriate only to scientific
theories. Nevertheless Dr Eysenck does continue to apply
such criteria to psychoanalysis and many of his criticisms
are good and very much to the point. Curiously enough,
having reduced his opponent to pulp, having declared
that 'psychoanalysis as a self-contained system claiming
to afford a scientific view of human nature is dead' (p. 232)
(although earlier he has said that 'The psychologist
knows no more about "human nature" than the next

---

* On this important point see the admirable lecture 'On clinical
medicine', by Sir Francis Walshe published in *The Lancet*, 16 December
1950, p. 781; also the article 'The methodology of clinical science', by
Sir James Spence, *The Lancet*, 26 September 1953, p. 629.

man') the author relents somewhat at the end of the chapter and even makes amends for his wholesale destructive criticism. He says he does not want to condemn psychoanalysis 'hook, line and sinker'. He confesses that 'Like most psychologists, I appreciate the breath of fresh air which Freud introduced into the musty dry-as-dust atmosphere of nineteenth century academic psychology. The brilliance of his mind has opened doors which no one would now wish to close again, and his keen insight has given us a storehouse of theories and hypotheses which will keep researchers busy for many years to come. All this one can appreciate without accepting the totality of his views as revelations from a higher authority, and without losing one's critical sense.' But according to the view of this essay to keep researchers busy is the chief scientific role of explanatory hypotheses; and to treat them as revelations from a higher authority is just as much a mistake in physics as it is in psychology.

Psychoanalysis is first and foremost a technique for helping certain types of sick people. If it is successful in doing this the explanatory hypotheses associated with it are of secondary importance. But it is extremely difficult to discover how successful it is. Dr Eysenck, in an earlier chapter of the same book, makes a devastating attack on psychotherapy in general. On the basis of what he admits to be imperfect data he takes a very gloomy view. He then turns to consider how a more adequate investigation could be carried out. He points out that it would be necessary to have a control group 'left without treatment for a given period'. Then in spite of his doubts he says: 'Can we justify the withholding of therapy, however insecurely it may be based, and however little we may know about its effects, from the person who is actually suffering at the moment?' For the method by which Dr Eysenck proposes to overcome this difficulty the reader must be referred to his book.

Freud's hypotheses were by no means all confined to those which were suggested by clinical observations. I should agree with Dr Eysenck that there is a tendency to over-generalize the results obtained and to apply them too dogmatically to social problems. Faults of this kind are not characteristic only of psychoanalysis but are found in many sciences. Freud also indulged in phylo-genetic speculation. By this I mean that he invented hypotheses involving assumptions concerning historical events far back in time and beyond the limits of any one individual life. Now there is a great danger connected with such speculations. It is connected with the difficulty of testing them. When once such a hypothesis becomes accepted (owing to the cleverness or prestige of its inven-tor) it is very difficult to refute it. This is especially the case in psychology, because there are no fossil motives! Even in palaeontology it is difficult to test such hypo-theses owing to the scarcity of material. But at least incidents like that of the Piltdown skull occur from time to time to restrain the exuberance of palaeontologists. Freud began his work at a time when phylogenetic hypo-theses were at the height of fashion; it was therefore very natural that he should have indulged in them.

In admitting phylogenetic hypotheses into psychology we are in danger of allowing ourselves to be influenced by a tacit assumption which I will call the evolutionary principle. It may be formulated as follows: *Nothing must be allowed to persons which cannot be regarded as 'nothing but' or 'a modified form of' something subhuman.*

If this principle is admitted and taken seriously we could never reach psychology at all. Because the lower animals cannot talk our languages and therefore cannot provide us with psychological data. This principle may be responsible for the curious attitude towards love which we find in scientific circles. In spite of nearly 2000 years of Christian teaching the importance of love in human affairs has only recently begun to be recognized in scientific writing.* This may be partly an effect of the finger and thumb philosophy but it may also be partly an outcome of the evolutionary principle. If you look in the index of a book on psychology you will often find that the word 'love' is missing, but you will usually find the word 'sex'. There seems to be a tendency to identify love with sex or at least to derive the former from the latter by means of a phylogenetic hypothesis. It would seem that because apes and monkeys copulate sex is felt to be scientifically respectable (you can write reports about it). Whether apes and monkeys love one another is more

* See I. D. Suttie, *The Origins of Love and Hate* (1935); John Bowlby, *Child Care and the Growth of Love* (Pelican Books, 1953). The following passage will give some notion of a modern attitude: 'The infant is helpless, entirely dependent on the mother for food, warmth and comfort, and the mother finds happiness in giving these services together with lavish affection and much physical contact. It has been demonstrated in numerous studies and in the experience of those who have worked with infants that the child who is deprived of the emotional warmth and comfort of personalized love is handicapped so seriously as to be vulnerable for the rest of his life. The movement away from institutions toward foster home care for dependent infants and small children is based on the demonstrated fact that while proper diet and fine physical care are essential, there is another ingredient that must be included for the well-being of the developing infant. This ingredient—the consistent and continuous love of a mother person—is less tangible than a carefully balanced formula or the asepsis of a nursery cubicle, but without it the personality of the child may be stunted. In this connection several pediatricians and psychiatrists pointed out the growing tendency to prescribe T.L.C. for small children on pediatric wards and in nurseries. T.L.C. means Tender Loving Care, a prescription which nurses are happy to fill now that the taboos against such contacts are being lifted.' This passage (which illustrates the difficulties of the finger and thumb philosophy) is from *Public Health is People*, a report on ' an institute on mental health in public health' held at Berkeley, California, 1948, by Ethel Ginsberg, published by the Commonwealth Fund, New York, 1950.

difficult to discover because they cannot talk well enough. The evolutionary principle then comes into operation with the hypothesis that love is copulation in disguise.

In this connexion also it is perhaps worth while to draw attention to the following passage in William James's *Principles of Psychology*, vol. 1, p. 140. It illustrates the way in which D_1 and D_2 can be smuggled into the picture in evolutionary arguments:

We talk, it is true, when we are darwinizing, as if the mere *body* that owns the brain had interests; we speak about the utilities of its various organs and how they help or hinder the body's survival; and we treat the survival as if it were an absolute end, existing as such in the physical world, a sort of actual *should-be*, presiding over the animal and judging his reactions, quite apart from the presence of any commenting intelligence outside. We forget that in the absence of some such super-added commenting intelligence (whether it be that of the animal itself, or only ours or Mr Darwin's), the reactions cannot be properly talked of as 'useful' or 'hurtful' at all. Considered merely physically, all that can be said of them is that *if* they occur in a certain way survival will as a matter of fact prove to be their incidental consequence. The organs themselves, and all the rest of the physical world, will, however, all the time be quite indifferent to this consequence, and would quite as cheerfully, the circumstances changed, compass the animal's destruction. In a word, survival can enter into a purely physiological discussion only as an *hypothesis made by an onlooker* about the future, but the moment you bring a consciousness into the midst, survival ceases to be a mere hypothesis. No longer is it, '*if* survival is to occur, then so and so must brain and other organs work'. It has now become an imperative decree: 'Survival *shall* occur, and therefore organs *must* so work!' *Real* ends appear for the first time now upon the world's stage.*

* See the reference to ends on p. 52.

But it is not uncommon to find in behaviourist writings racial survival spoken of as a *need* of an individual organism, like the need for air or for water.

In the book already referred to, Dr Eysenck gives an example of an experimental falsification of one of Freud's hypotheses concerning dreams. The following is interesting as a falsification of a generalization of Freud regarding unsatisfied appetite:

Freud once said: 'Try and subject a number of very strongly differentiated human beings to the same amount of starvation. With the increase of the imperative need for food all individual differences will be blotted out, and, in their place, we shall see the uniform expression of the unsatisfied instinct.' But in the concentration camps we witnessed the contrary, we saw how, faced with the identical situation, one man became a swine while the other attained almost saintly status. And Robert J. Lifton (1954, *Amer. J. Psychiat.*, **110**, 733) writes about American soldiers in North Korean prisoner-of-war camps: 'There were examples among them both of altruistic behaviour as well as the most primitive forms of struggle for survival.'*

Dr Eysenck's criticisms of Freud were introduced in the first place by way of an example of the undesirability of applying to a young science which is struggling for recognition the same severe standards of criticism which would be appropriate to one which is well established. As an example this has been complicated by the fact that Freud's ingenuity led him to invent hypotheses outside his strictly clinical experience and to apply them beyond the domain of therapeutics. Such hypotheses are therefore exposed to general criticism and I have had no choice but to agree with Dr Eysenck's remarks about them.

* Viktor E. Frankl, 'The Concept of Man in Psychotherapy', *Proceedings of the Royal Society of Medicine*, vol. 47 (1954), p. 975.

Turning now to other critics of psychology it has sometimes been brought forward as a defect of this science, and as a reason for withholding a knowledge of it from medical students, that it has too many conflicting hypotheses. But according to the third policy maxim mentioned on p. 37 this abundance of hypotheses (if they are good ones, and this can be discovered only by trying them) should be a matter for congratulation rather than regret. It will be a difficulty from the teaching point of view only if the duty of the teacher is conceived to be the inculcation of a single dogma. The existence of more than one hypothesis encourages the habit of critical reflection and focuses attention on the observational level which is the common groundwork for all the hypotheses. The task of the teacher will certainly be eased when a genius with the requisite clinical experience comes along and combines what is best in the existing hypotheses into a single theory. Psychology is sometimes condemned on account of the lunatic fringe of cranks, quacks and other camp followers which is said to accompany it. But this does not distinguish psychology from other sciences. They too have their camp followers: astronomy has its astrologers, chemistry its alchemists and neurology its phrenologists.

A peculiarity of psychology has been pointed out by Professor Notcutt in the book which has already been mentioned; on p. 147 he writes:

It must be emphasized that there are at present no psychological laws in most regions of behaviour, in spite of the immense efforts that have gone into formulating them. This is not usually made obvious because psychologists do not like running down their own subject. . . . The public expects the psychologist to possess general laws of a cause-and-effect kind. The way in which psychology has been boosted as a natural science has encouraged the public to suppose that such laws exist, where in fact they do not.*

Whether or not it should be called a 'general law of a cause-and-effect kind' a familiar and perfectly good psychological law is expressed in the following words:

Every person strives to maximize his or her self-esteem.

The impulse with which this law is concerned provides the basis of human conceit, of which quality there is abundance. We see it in the very title—*Homo sapiens*—which we have bestowed upon ourselves, for of all qualities wisdom is surely the rarest among human beings. It is a plausible hypothesis that a great many of our troubles are traceable to this impulse in those individuals who are only able to maximize their self-esteem at the expense of others, from the world-scale conflicts which are set in motion by Napoleons or Hitlers to the petty but harrowing squabbles of everyday domestic life. This impulse also appears to play a part in retarding the development of science. When a new hypothesis is suggested it may threaten the prestige of those whose pet hypotheses are endangered or, if the new ideas can only be understood after careful study, people who find this difficult will also be confronted with a shock to their self-esteem. The importance of prestige and propaganda in promoting new hypotheses is indicated in the following passage:

prestige is a very wonderful and powerful thing. Mr Winston Churchill is reported to have said that the essentials of persuasive and convincing speech-making were three in number. In order of importance, he said, they were: first, who you are; second, how you say it; third, what you say.†

* *The Psychology of Personality* (1953).
† H. Yellowlees, *To Define True Madness* (1953), p. 39.

Another reference to the impulse to maximization of one's self-esteem is made on p. 98 of the same book: '. . . one of the easiest ways of maintaining a good opinion of oneself is to hold a low opinion of those around one, so Mr X often becomes a devastatingly destructive critic of others.' We shall see examples of this later.

Two devices are in common use in connexion with the impulse to maximize our self-esteem. First, that of *paying lip service*, by which we achieve an appearance of conforming to standards which are considered praiseworthy but which we find inconvenient in practice. Second, *rationalization*, by which we explain away to our own satisfaction discrepancies between our professed principles and our practice. In this way we blind ourselves: in the moral sphere to our misdeeds, in the intellectual sphere to our ignorance. Blindness of the first kind blocks the road to salvation; blindness of the second kind closes the door to discovery.

Meanwhile the subject of causal laws calls for a separate section. We shall see that even outside psychology we are frequently satisfied with causal laws which fall short of perfection.

§ 14. CAUSES AND CAUSAL LAWS

ON the whole it seems to be advisable to talk about causal laws rather than about causes in scientific literature. The notion of cause is commonly used in medical literature in much the same way in which it is used in everyday language, and this has certain disadvantages. Such phrases, for example, as 'the cause of cancer' or 'the cause of jaundice' have the disadvantage not only of suggesting that cancer or jaundice is a single entity, but also of suggesting that there is some one thing which can be said to cause cancer or jaundice and that it is the business of medical research to find this thing. This suggestion is unfortunate because natural science is not so much a search for 'the cause of so-and-so' as a search for causal laws, and causal laws (especially in the biological sciences) always involve a complex of factors each one of which has as good a claim to the title of 'cause' as any other. The phrase 'the cause of so-and-so' has the effect of emphasizing some one factor at the expense of the others, sometimes with unfortunate results. For example, if we say that the tubercle bacillus is the cause of tuberculosis we may suggest that the presence of tubercle bacilli in the body is a sufficient condition for the occurrence of tuberculosis. But we know that this is not the case. A person can have tubercle bacilli in his body without having tuberculosis. On the other hand we should not say that a person was suffering from tuberculosis if he did *not* have, and never had, tubercle bacilli in his body. We may say, therefore, that the presence of tubercle bacilli in a person's body is a *necessary* condition, but we cannot say that it is a *sufficient* condition for the occurrence of tuberculosis. We can say that it is *a* factor or *a* cause but not *the* cause. We could only speak strictly of *the* cause if we could specify *all* the conditions that must be satisfied if a person is to fall a victim to tuberculosis. In order to have a strict causal law we require a statement which specifies not only what conditions are *necessary* for the production of a certain result, but also what conditions are *sufficient* to do this.

Let us consider another example. Suppose we represent the whole life of a man—from fertilization to funeral—by a straight line segment, the points of which will represent *instants* in the man's life, and let us stipulate that when one instant is *earlier* than another the point representing it is to lie to the *left* of the point representing the other.

Let us call the whole piece of the life between and including any two points or instants a *time-stretch* of that life. Let us say that one time-stretch *adjoins* another if (as in the diagram) the last moment of the first (or x in the diagram) is also the first moment of the second (or y in the diagram). (Among other possible relations we can have overlapping and also a gap between x and y; but for simplicity in what follows we shall confine attention to adjoining.)

Now time-stretches can be classified in various ways according to what is happening in them. For example, there will be time-stretches of persons during which a person is swallowing an emetic and there will be time-stretches during which that same person is vomiting. Let us for brevity denote by 'E' the class of all time-stretches of persons during the whole of which they are drinking an emetic, and let us use 'V' similarly for the class of all time-stretches during which the person is vomiting. Also let us use the Greek letter epsilon to express class-membership, so that instead of writing 'the time-stretch x is a member of E' we can write more briefly '$x \varepsilon E$'. Similarly let us use the expression 'xAy' as an abbreviation for the statement 'the time-stretch x adjoins the time-stretch y'. If it is understood that the letters 'x' and 'y' represent any time-stretches of persons we can use them without the prefix 'the time-stretch'. Now we can express our causal law as follows. We can say:

Whatever time-stretch x may be

if $x \varepsilon E$ then there is a y such that xAy and $y \varepsilon V$;

in other words, every emetic-swallowing stretch is immediately followed by a vomiting stretch. If we find that this happens whenever we try it we shall be inclined to say that swallowing an emetic is a sufficient condition for the occurrence of vomiting. What will be required if we are to be able to say that swallowing an emetic is a necessary condition for this to happen? We must find that the following generalization holds:

Whatever time-stretch x may be

if not $(x \varepsilon E)$ then there is no y such that $x A y$ and $y \varepsilon V$;

in other words, if a time-stretch is not an emetic-swallowing stretch, then it does not adjoin a vomiting stretch. And there is clearly no such law, because we know from experience that people sometimes vomit even when they have not taken an emetic. Consequently we do not in this case have a strict causal law. We have a law stating the sufficient conditions but not one stating the necessary conditions. Such a law may be useful enough for most purposes, but it cannot strictly be regarded as a causal law.

It is interesting to inquire more closely why it is that a law which gives *only* the necessary or *only* the sufficient conditions, instead of both, cannot strictly be called a causal law. This is a point which is not always made clear in discussions of this subject, so it deserves a little further attention. Instead of restricting attention to the particular classes E and V, let us treat the problem quite generally by using the letters 'X' 'Y' and 'Z' to represent any classes of time-stretches of persons in which we may be interested. Now suppose that observation seems to us to justify us in asserting the generalization:

Whatever time-stretch x may be

if $x \varepsilon X$ then there is a y such that $x A y$ and $y \varepsilon Y$ (1)

but that when we have not $(x \varepsilon X)$ and xAy sometimes we have $y \varepsilon Y$ and sometimes not $(y \varepsilon Y)$. Then we can say that being an X and adjoining a time-stretch is a sufficient but not a necessary condition for obtaining a Y.

This state of affairs might be brought about in the following way. Suppose that there is another class Z not yet recognized by the experimenter but which in fact gives, for any time-stretch x

$$\text{if } x \varepsilon Z \text{ then there is a } y \text{ such that } xAy \text{ and } y \varepsilon Y \quad (2)$$

and also

for any time-stretch x

$$\text{if not } (x \varepsilon Z) \text{ then there is no } y \text{ such that } xAy \text{ and } y \varepsilon Y \quad (3)$$

and let us further suppose that the class X is a sub-class of the class Z so that every member of X is also a member of Z but not vice versa. On this assumption it is clear that when we experiment with members of X we shall get (1), but with an x which does not belong to X there will be two possibilities: it will belong to Z or it will not belong to Z. If it belongs to Z and we have a y such that xAy then

by (2) we shall obtain $y \varepsilon Y$; but if it belongs to not-Z then by (3) we should obtain not $(y \varepsilon Y)$. The hypothesis regarding Z thus explains why we do not have a strict causal law in terms of X. At the same time the law (1) may be very useful in practice, it would be pedantic in the extreme to reject it because it is not a complete causal law. Moreover further investigation may reveal the strict causal law in terms of Z.

Now consider the case where we have, for any time-stretch x

if not $(x \varepsilon X)$ then there is no y such that xAy and $y \varepsilon Y$ (4)

but we do *not* have (for any time-stretch x)

if $x \varepsilon X$ then there is a y such that xAy and $y \varepsilon Y$ (5)

so that the occurrence of an X is a necessary but not a sufficient condition for obtaining $y \varepsilon Y$. Such a state of affairs would be realized if we have a class Z such that only when an x belongs both to X *and* to Z do we get $y \varepsilon Y$ if xAy. In this case the things which do not belong to X will either belong to Z or not to Z and in both cases one of the factors required for getting $y \varepsilon Y$ will be missing so we shall always get not $(y \varepsilon Y)$ in agreement with (4). On the other hand, some members of X will belong to not (Z) and these will not give $y \varepsilon Y$, so that we do not have (5).*

The foregoing considerations are also illustrated by the rules commonly known in bacteriology as Koch's Postulates, which prescribe 'the kind of evidence which will

* More commonly, perhaps, in the biological sciences and in psychology, causal laws will be formulated with the help of expressions of the form 'p per cent of Xs adjoin members of Y'. Their analysis and criticism require the theory of sampling. I have confined my attention to the type discussed in the text solely in the interests of simplicity. A better way of expressing causal laws is by means of the notion of *environment*, but this also is too complicated for the purpose of the present essay. See my *Biology and Language* (1952), p. 208, note 8. In the formulations in the text it is also tacitly assumed (again in the interests of simplicity) that the time-stretch x is always followed by another one, i.e. that the life concerned does not end with the end of x.

justify the conclusion that a particular disease is caused by a particular parasite', namely:

(1) The organism should be found in all cases of the disease in question and its distribution in the body should be in accordance with the lesions observed.

(2) The organism should be cultivated outside the body of the host, in pure culture, for several generations.

(3) The organism so isolated should reproduce the disease in other susceptible animals.*

In (1) and (3) the reader will recognize rules corresponding to the two parts of our causal law. If (1) is satisfied the presence of the organism is a necessary condition, if (3) is satisfied the presence of the organism in question in a susceptible animal constitutes a sufficient condition for the development of the disease. (What is meant here by 'susceptible', other than not immune, is an interesting but difficult question.)

In R. W. Fairbrother, *A Text-book of Bacteriology* (7th ed., 1953), p. 8, we read: 'While the fulfilment of all these criteria is not considered necessary at the present time for establishing the relationship of an organism to a particular disease, their value in checking preposterous claims by inexperienced workers has been considerable.' This is a highly interesting remark in the present context because it seems to illustrate my point that less stringent rules of criticism are applied to orthodox than to unorthodox hypotheses. It means that bacteriologists are usually satisfied with something short of strict causal laws. When therefore psychologists are criticized by very strict

* See Topley and Wilson's *Principles of Bacteriology and Immunity*, 3rd ed. (1947), vol. II, p. 1002, where, referring to these postulates it is stated that 'there is no clear evidence that Koch ever enunciated them in the categorical form in which they are usually quoted'.

criteria they can take comfort from the thought that other sciences too are satisfied with something short of perfection.

Although there may be few laws in psychology when this science is judged by the strictest standards, yet we do in fact, in our everyday life, employ rough and ready rules regarding the way in which people will behave, and the success of advertising agents and propaganda ministers in totalitarian states shows what can be done (if that is the sort of thing you want to do) with the means already at our disposal. But the task of medicine is to restore sick people to health or, if possible, to prevent them from becoming sick, and this task is by no means identical with the task of predicting the behaviour of persons.*

Meanwhile there is still more to be said on the subject of causal laws. In the traditional causal laws, examples of which have now been examined, *whenever* a member of a certain class is in a certain spatio-temporal relation to another thing, that thing belongs to a certain other class. Now in the biological world we frequently encounter situations which are quite different from this; namely, those in which *each time* a certain antecedent $x \varepsilon X$ occurs we get a *different* result, instead of always the same one. Instead of 'same cause, same effect' it is 'same cause, different effect'. This is well illustrated by the immunization process. In the field of behaviour it is sufficiently familiar to have become embodied in a proverb: The burnt child dreads the fire. In a more sophisticated form it is exemplified by the conditioned reflexes. The occurrence of such processes does not of course mean the abandonment of causal laws; it only means that in the

* In psychotherapy the patient is not passive. Treatment will not be successful unless the patient is willing to admit that he is ill and tries to get better. See also below, pp. 112 *et seq.*

biological sciences we must be prepared to find causal laws, or generalizations resembling causal laws, of a special and complicated kind.*

But it also has other consequences, and an examination of a simple example will bring out a difference between psychology and neurology which is relevant to the present inquiry. We can take the proverb just mentioned, at the same time expressing it in a manner which is more in accordance with scientific usage. Also let us change 'dreads' into 'avoids' in order to make it easier to treat from a purely neurological point of view and to make the comparison with psychology clearer. Let us formulate our law as follows:

Every child that has been burnt avoids fires.

If we are now given two singular statements:

(i) Tom is a child,
(ii) Tom has been burnt,

then, with the help of our law we can predict:

(iii) Tom avoids fires.

---

* Here it is interesting to recall the remark of Lord Russell which was quoted on p. 34: 'It is not the uniformity of nature that should surprise us, for, by sufficient analytical ingenuity, any conceivable course of nature might be shown to exhibit uniformity. What should surprise us is the fact that the uniformity is simple enough for us to be able to discover it.' When we consider the enormous part that has been played in physics by mathematics in helping it to discover and express its relatively simple laws, the thought suggests itself that the paucity of laws in psychology may be partly the result of insufficient 'analytical ingenuity' and partly of the absence at present of appropriate mathematical techniques. Ordinary language can cope only with comparatively simple problems. There is also another aspect to this state of affairs, namely that the lack of laws in psychology may be a blessing in disguise. When we consider what can be done by propaganda with our present psychological knowledge we are reminded of George Orwell's *1984* and of the horrors that might be perpetrated through the misuse of more perfect psychological laws.

The initial conditions (i) and (ii) present no great difficulty from the psychological point of view. We can satisfy ourselves about the truth of (i) by getting views, sounds, feels, etc., of Tom. Regarding (ii) we can ask Tom whether he has been burnt or, if he is too young, we can ask his parents or nurse. The answers we get will not be one hundred per cent reliable; but nothing ever is. Tom or his parents or nurse may have forgotten; or he may have been burnt when no one was near and the painful memory may have been repressed, or any one of those concerned may have some motive for not telling the truth. But in spite of all these difficulties we habitually and successfully make use of such generalizations in everyday life.

But now let us turn to see how the matter is treated from the neurological angle. Neurology has no use for 'same cause, different effect'; it has recourse to a device to restore the *status quo* and to give us a law of the traditional 'same cause, same effect' type. But it can only do this with the help of an explanatory hypothesis, the hypothesis, namely, that some time-stretches at least of the afferent torrent of nervous impulses which is perpetually traversing each brain during life leave behind them enduring traces, so that when a similar torrent passes through again it passes through a different kind of brain, each kind of brain having a different law. Let us use '*B*' to denote the class of all human brains belonging to persons who have been burnt. Then we shall require the following hypotheses:

(iv) All persons who have been burnt have a brain of kind *B*. (This is merely a restatement of the definition of '*B*'.)

(v) Whenever a person is in the presence of hot objects efferent torrents excited by them are traversing his brain.

(vi) Every person whose brain is of type B and is being traversed by an afferent torrent excited by hot objects also has a brain from which an efferent torrent is passing to result in movements by which hot objects are avoided.

To test these hypotheses we require such singular statements as:

(vii) Tom has been burnt.
(viii) Tom is in the presence of hot objects.

From (iv), (v), (vi), (vii) and (viii) it follows that Tom is avoiding hot objects. In order to obtain (vii) we must ask Tom or his parents or nurse the same question which we asked in the case of the psychological law. We cannot independently discover whether Tom's brain is a B or not. Even if we could specify the structure of members of B in terms of the neurone hypothesis we could not, by opening Tom's skull and examining his brain, discover whether it was a B or not. (And if we could, the making of such an additional observation would interfere too much with the original experiment.) As Lord Russell has remarked, you cannot by examining a man's brain tell whether he speaks French or has visited New York. Until these difficulties are overcome, neurology must have recourse to psychological data and methods in the sense in which (vii) is a psychological datum. I mention this not to detract from neurological hypotheses, but simply to show that their observational basis may not be so very different from one which is couched in psychological terms and therefore shares with the latter any difficulties it may have.

Perhaps the chief reason why causal laws are difficult to find and even classificatory generalizations are rare in connexion with persons and living organisms in general is the occurrence of a process of development. This process is so extraordinary that when it was first investigated in the modern world the tendency among the learned was to deny its occurrence and explain it away.* They preferred the fantastic hypothesis that the entire *Homo sapiens* was hierarchically encapsulated in the ovaries of Adam's Eve rather than accept such an extraordinary thing. (Let this be a warning to all who put *erklärende* psychology before *verstehende* psychology!) Now that it has become more familiar and we have the notion of self-duplicating units like cells, the process does not seem so extraordinary, although embryology is still a rather backward subject from the theoretical point of view. We have a great many generalizations of observation records in this science but few impressive explanatory hypotheses. But what makes things difficult is not only the occurrence of a process of development, but the fact that this process is subject throughout its course to environmental influences accompanied by the complications discussed in the preceding paragraph. Moreover, the starting points of the several developments (the fertilized ova in the case of persons) are not all alike. At all events we have grounds for the hypothesis that there are many different kinds of zygote. There are also very many different kinds of environment. From these two circumstances there result a very great variety of persons, presenting great difficulties for the classifier and law finder. From the medical point of view there is yet another difficulty. One person may differ from another in a way that may seem trivial to a disinterested onlooker, but may be very important to the happiness of the person concerned. Also, in the case of persons, the environment will be partly a social environment with all the complications and subtleties which this

* See above p. 32.

entails, so that a single word may have an enormous effect. Another feature of the development process which is especially important from the psychological standpoint is this: it has, metaphorically speaking, a magnifying effect like the beam from a projection lantern. If you hold an opaque object in the beam the nearer it is to the lantern the greater is its effect on the picture on the screen. There is something analogous to this in development. The nearer to the beginning of development a noxious factor operates the more serious the effect on later stages. This generalization, like all biological generalizations, needs qualification. In some organisms, especially in the early stages, regulative processes may intervene to correct an abnormality, but in the absence of such processes the generalization holds. It seems to hold also in the psychological domain. Perhaps it is for this reason that events in early childhood, although unnoticed at the time, may have serious effects in later life. Whether they do or not will depend not only on the sort of zygote from which the development begins, and on the occurrence of regulative processes, but also on another feature of person development, namely the occurrence of crises at certain periods of the process. Thus we have the crisis of birth, the crisis of weaning (both nutritional and personal), the crisis of leaving home for school and school for the larger world, followed by the crises attending falling in love with someone outside the family, getting married, becoming a parent, and so on. These are times when the forgotten pathogenic experiences of early infancy may show their effects. But we are still only at the beginning of learning about these things.

All these considerations lead us to expect that the class of persons is a highly diversified one, and when, with this in mind, we consider that each clinical psychologist examines a different sample of this population, when we remember that his own preferences and prejudices will enter into his attitude to what he observes, shall we not rather be surprised that alternative hypotheses are so few than regret that there are so many?

Finally are we not perhaps overlooking the most obvious point of all? May it not be that our naïve intuitions are not so far wrong after all and that casual laws in relation to persons are few or of restricted extension because persons are not entirely subject to them? In our daily life we distinguish between strong-minded and weak-minded persons. On the whole we admire and respect the former more than the latter and it is presumably part of the business of the clinical psychologist to help his patients to be strong-minded. We think of a strong-minded person as one who is master of his surroundings and of his primitive impulses (always of course within certain limits), as something in fact that is the very antithesis of a machine waiting to have its buttons pressed. If this is accepted, then perhaps what is wanted is an exploration of other possible lines of approach as alternatives to the traditional one by way of causal laws, ones which will render people not more but less amenable to propaganda.

In thus appealing to naïve intuition we are simply doing the same in regard to the psychological domain that we have already done for the physical. We saw in §7 that we were compelled to let our faith in $D_3 - D_1$ rest on our naïve intuitions of a physical world which we find ourselves already possessed of as soon as we begin to reflect. Corresponding remarks apply to D_1. If we stubbornly refuse to accept these intuitions, we may be making a mistake analogous to that of the eighteenth-century embryologists who refused to accept what they saw through their microscopes.

§ 15. SUBJECTIVE AND OBJECTIVE

SOME words carry with them an aura of respectability and approval, so that even people who do not believe in what they stand for use them in order to shine by their reflected glory. Familiar examples from the field of politics are 'democracy' and 'liberty'. Other words have such a bad odour that they have become almost like swear words. To the first category belongs 'objective' and to the second 'subjective' and 'introspection'. The word 'objective' seems frequently to be used as though it were synonymous with 'scientific'. 'Subjective' is used as though to express the very antithesis of what is objective, as though merely to whisper the word 'subjective' in connexion with a doctrine would be enough to condemn it. If therefore psychology deals with what is subjective, it would seem to stand condemned from the start from the point of view of scientific respectability. 'Introspection' is also supposed to have a bad connotation and its alleged special association with psychology is sometimes used as a ground for condemning the latter.

What are we to say to this? Let us try to discover how these words are used when they are used seriously and apart from judgments about whether what we are applying them to is or is not to be called scientific. It is commonly assumed that all things belonging to D_2 are subjective in the sense of personal. That is to say it is assumed that not only is my angry feeling distinct from your angry feeling, and my toothache from yours, but my view of the sea is distinct from your view of the sea, and my sound of a bell distinct from yours. However much the things making up these pairs may resemble one another, it is assumed that they are distinct. But the subjectivity of these things does not prevent us from communicating about them. I remember wondering as a child, when I heard adults talking about their headaches, how I should know when I had a headache. But when the time came there was no difficulty. Moreover, as we have seen, if all the things in D_2 are in this sense subjective, then the views and tactual feels upon which we rely so much in natural science for the testing of statements concerning D_3 are also subjective. The important point of difference here between the physical sciences and psychology is not that what is got is objective in one case and subjective in the other, but that in the first case the subjectively got is helped to objectivity by both doing and talking, in the second case only by talking. The surgeon and the physician both use their fingers as well as talk, the medical psychologist only uses talk.

But apart from this sense of 'subjective' there is another one. Very often we hear a person or an opinion condemned as subjective. In this case what is meant is that the person is biased or that the opinion has been reached under the influence of some strong feeling. The word 'emotional' is also sometimes used in this sense. 'Emotion' is another of those bad words which are used to express disapproval. To be emotional is supposed to be the antithesis of being scientific. Not that the man of science is supposed to be devoid of emotions, but that he is supposed to have them much more under control than ordinary mortals. It is not very difficult to be calm and unemotional when we are dealing with balls running down inclined planes or when we are mixing harmless solutions in a test tube. It would not therefore be surprising to find that in the physical sciences judgments do not often get mixed up with feelings. But when we come to deal with persons it is much more difficult to be impartial or at least to exclude feelings. I shall now give an example of the way in which personal bias can enter into a scientific discussion. This is not an example from psychological writing, it is from an article by an eminent biologist on variation in animals and plants. It might seem at first sight that such a topic would be unlikely to provide opportunity or temptation for the introduction of personal prejudice. But in this article we find the following passage:

For some reason there is a huge body of folk-lore about correlation. Red-haired people are believed to be quick-tempered, high-browed men to be intelligent, and so on. These particular beliefs do little harm. Similar beliefs about the psychological characters correlated with dark skins and hooked noses have been responsible for millions of deaths.

It seems clear from this passage that the author holds that beliefs which are responsible for millions of deaths are harmful and that it is not improper to say so in a biological article which is supposed to be objective and devoid of value judgments. Many people, who might otherwise dis-approve of the intrusion of such judgments into writing belonging to natural science would nevertheless be pre-pared to forgive this particular lapse from scientific objectivity. They would regard this remark simply as the expression of the kindly feelings of a benevolent old gentle-man which will not detract from his scientific work. But then the reader may recall that four pages back the article contained the following passage:

This notion of a fruitful conflict, which Darwin applied to the struggle for life both within a species and between species, can thus be applied not only to evolution but to its prerequisite, genetical variation. This seems to be in accord with dialectical materialism, as developed by Lenin (1915). However, at the present time the majority of the followers of Lenin take a different view.

This passage clearly puts a new and sinister complexion on the other one. It cannot be because they are responsible for millions of deaths that the author regards certain beliefs as harmful, but for some other reason. For the doctrines of Lenin have, since 1917, also been responsible for millions of deaths. Thus it is not the millions of deaths that is objected to; it is the kind of people who are killed and the kind of people who do the killing that is important. If you approve of the people killed but disapprove of the people who do the killing, then it is harmful. But if you approve of the people who do the killing and disapprove of those who are killed, then it is not harmful, it is a fruitful conflict. Thus not only value judgments, but political bias also, enter into a piece of scientific writing in this example, although it is not from a work on psychology. Another point is also illustrated, namely the way in which language enables us to give things alternative names that permit them to enter places from which they might otherwise be excluded. 'Fruitful struggle' sounds so much nicer than 'killing'.

Connected with this second sense of 'subjective' is the widespread human activity called *despising* which is sometimes directed against psychology and psychologists. It seems to be an aspect of the almost universal urge of persons to maximize their self-esteem. One way of doing this is by despising other persons. I propose to describe a particularly sad case of this complaint, the victim being an eminent mathematician at one of our ancient universities. During his retirement he wrote a book about mathematics. But he was so ashamed of doing this that he devoted quite a number of pages to apologizing for it. In fact he begins the book with the words: 'It is a melancholy experience for a professional mathematician to find himself writing about mathematics.' This at least has the merit, which an opening sentence should have, of whetting the reader's appetite. Why in the world, the un-sophisticated reader may ask, should it be a melancholy experience for an eminent professional mathematician to find himself writing about mathematics? And why, if he felt so sad about it, did he do it? The surprising answer to the first question is quickly given: it is beneath his dignity! 'The function of a mathematician is to do something, to prove new theorems, and not to talk about what he or other mathematicians have done.' The author then goes on to explain (and here we come to the crux of the matter) that people who write about mathematics are inferior persons who are to be despised by all right and high-minded mathematicians. He then generalizes over a wide range of human occupations. He says:

Statesmen despise publicists, painters despise art-critics, and physiologists, physicists, or mathematicians have usually similar feelings; there is no scorn more profound, or on the whole more justifiable, than that of the men who make for the men who explain. Exposition, criticism, appreciation, is work for second-rate minds.

What an amazing outburst of nonsense from a learned man! Especially from one who himself wrote a well-known expository text-book of mathematics! That all this despising goes on I have no doubt; what is surprising is that anyone should applaud it! It is one thing to write *Hamlet*, and it is another thing to write a book about *Hamlet*, as Dr Dover Wilson has done; and just as *Hamlet* itself is a good thing so a book about *Hamlet* may also be a good thing. Why on earth should we despise a person whose writing enhances our enjoyment of a good thing? Each product is to be judged on its own merits and by the canons of criticism appropriate to it and not on its relation to the other. One is a play and the other is not a play, and the possibility is not excluded that a book about a play may, of its kind, be an even greater achievement than the play about which it is written. There seems to be no justification for the assumption that one must *always* be inferior to the other, still less that the author of one must always be despised. This is not to assert that all literary criticism is good or of a high order. But neither is all poetry good or of a high order. To be a poet is not necessarily to be a good poet and to be a critic is not necessarily to be a bad critic. But if we lay it down as a dogma that literary (or any other) criticism is 'work for second-rate minds', then of course we shall always suppose without inquiry that the product of their efforts is also second rate and we shall not condescend to inquire whether in fact our generalization is confirmed. In the same way, a book about mathematics belongs to a different science from mathematics itself (it is now called metamathematics), but it need not be in any way inferior of its kind to a book of mathematics. Lord Russell has devoted a considerable part of his life to writing about mathematics, but I have never heard that he is to be despised for doing so.

But we have not finished with our disgruntled mathematician. He relates how he had at one time argued about this question with Housman the poet, who had in a lecture 'denied very emphatically that he was a "critic"', ' but he had denied it in what seemed to me a singularly perverse way, and had expressed an admiration for literary criticism which startled and scandalized me'. He then quotes a passage from the lecture, in which Housman had said:

In these twenty-two years I have improved in some respects and deteriorated in others, but I have not so much improved as to become a literary critic, nor so much deteriorated as to fancy that I have become one.

This seems plain enough, but our mathematician was so bent on despising critics that he could not believe that

Housman meant what he said. He found it so deplorable that, as he tells us, he decided to tackle Housman about it in hall. 'We argued these questions all through dinner, and I think that finally he agreed with me.' He does not, however, seem to have been entirely satisfied. He adds: 'There may have been some doubt about Housman's feelings, and I do not wish to claim him as on my side; but there is no doubt at all about the feelings of men of science, and I share them fully.' The hypothesis suggests itself that Housman was so bored with the conversation that he agreed in sheer self-defence in the hope of bringing it to an end. If what this mathematician says about men of science is correct, we can only hope that a little more reflexion will show that such an attitude is not compatible with the so-called rational attitude with which men of science are traditionally supposed to be endowed. All this muddled thinking seems to be the outcome of bad feeling, and the bad feeling—the despising of other persons—is perhaps the outcome of a wish to feel superior. By means of a dogma about critics we provide ourselves with a permanent supply of beings to whom we can feel superior. It is part of the deep-seated snobbishness of *Homo* (self-styled) *sapiens*.

When we find learned men belonging to the so-called exact sciences making asses of themselves, we shall take little heed when the charge of subjectivity (in the second sense) is levelled against psychology. Our example of the practice of despising those whose interests we do not happen to share shows how far we can fall short of the creed of the man of science which was expressed by the late Dr Mervyn Henry Gordon in the words:

It is the glory of a good bit of work that it opens the way for still better, and thus rapidly leads to its own eclipse. *The chief object of research is the advancement, not of the investigator, but of knowledge.**

* *The Lancet*, 8 August 1953, p. 300. Italic not in the original.

§ 16. FEELING

IT was mentioned in the last section that 'emotion' is another word which is supposed to have a bad connotation, especially from the scientific point of view. We are told that we must 'keep our emotions out of it', that we 'must not be emotional'. The impression one gets is that emotions are disreputable things which—like tonsils—we may be better without. Some of the people who tell us to 'keep our emotions out of it' also tell us (in other contexts) that emotions are only side effects or concomitants of cerebral processes over which we have no control because they obey unalterable laws. But in that case how are we to keep our emotions out of anything, and how do men of science contrive to keep their emotions so well under control? It is a little difficult to understand why so much fuss is made about emotion in such contexts because the fact that someone has reached a certain scientific belief under the influence of some strong feeling or prejudice does not in itself provide a basis for rejecting that belief any more than it does for accepting it. We check scientific statements by the agreement or otherwise of their logical consequences with observations, not by looking up the biographies of those who first proposed them in order to discover their emotional state at the time.

Throughout the period of time during which men have reflected about themselves there seems to have been an unresolved conflict between the life of the intellect and the life of feeling. The fact seems to be that in some people intellectual interests are stronger than emotional ones and in others the opposite is the case. The belief that they conflict has presumably been kept alive by the fondness for despising those whose interests do not coincide with our own, of which we saw an example in the last section. From a detached point of view there does not seem to be any reason why they should conflict. And yet there is a deep-seated tradition that one is superior to the other, so much so that until Freud appeared on the scene psychologists devoted little attention to feelings. This tradition is even reflected in the title we have bestowed upon ourselves in the zoological nomenclature.

Perhaps after all there is no genuine basis for such a conflict and its continuation has been a misfortune. Let us hear a witness on the side of feeling:

The exertions of Locke, Hume, Gibbon, Voltaire, Rousseau, and their disciples, in favour of oppressed and deluded humanity, are entitled to the gratitude of mankind. Yet it is easy to calculate the degree of moral and intellectual improvement which the world would have exhibited, had they never lived. A little more nonsense would have been talked for a century or two; and perhaps a few more men, women, and children, burnt as heretics. We might not at this moment have been congratulating each other on the abolition of the Inquisition in Spain. But it exceeds all imagination to conceive what would have been the moral condition of the world if neither Dante, Petrarch, Boccaccio, Chaucer, Shakespeare, Calderon, Lord Bacon, nor Milton, had ever existed; if Raphael and Michael Angelo had never been born; if the Hebrew poetry had never been translated; if a revival of the study of Greek literature had never taken place; if no monuments of ancient sculpture had been handed down to us; and if the poetry of the religion of the ancient world had been extinguished together with its belief. The human mind could never, except by the intervention of these excitements, have been awakened to the invention of the grosser sciences, and that application of analytical reasoning to the aberrations of society, which it is now attempted to exalt over the direct expression of the inventive and creative faculty itself.

This passage is from P. B. Shelley's *Defence of Poetry* (1821). (It is strange that he should have put Bacon among the poets. Lytton Strachey would have emphatically repudiated this classification.) Some critics will not be very much impressed by Shelley's argument. They will wonder how he could be so confident about what would have happened under the circumstances he describes in the absence of experiment. But there is more to come, which may have a bearing on our present troubles.

We have more moral, political and historical wisdom, than we know how to reduce into practice; we have more scientific and economical knowledge than can be accommodated to the just distribution of the produce which it multiplies. The poetry in these systems of thought, is concealed by the accumulation of facts and calculating processes. There is no want of knowledge respecting what is wisest and best in morals, government, and political economy, or at least, what is wiser and better than what men now practise and endure. But we let '*I dare not* wait upon *I would*, like the poor cat in the adage.' We want the creative faculty to imagine that which we know; we want the generous impulse to act that which we imagine; we want the poetry of life: our calculations have outrun conception; we have eaten more than we can digest. The cultivation of those sciences which have enlarged the limits of the empire of man over the external world, has, for want of the poetic faculty, proportionally circumscribed those of the internal world; and man, having enslaved the elements, remains himself a slave. To what but a cultivation of the mechanical arts in a degree disproportioned to the presence of the creative faculty, which is the basis of all knowledge, is to be attributed the abuse of all invention for abridging and combining labour, to the exasperation of the inequality of mankind? From what other cause has it arisen that the discoveries which should have lightened, have added a weight to the curse imposed on Adam? Poetry, and the principle of Self, of which money is the visible incarnation, are the God and Mammon of the world.

Lest Shelley has overstated his case let us hear one more witness who is not likely to be guilty of this error:

... I yet believe that, by sufficient restraint, there is an element of wisdom to be learned from the mystical way of feeling, which does not seem to be attainable in any other way. If this is the truth, mysticism is to be commended as an attitude towards life, not as a creed about the world. The metaphysical creed, I shall maintain, is a mistaken outcome of the emotion, although this emotion, as colouring and informing all other thoughts and feelings, is the inspirer of whatever is best in Man. Even the cautious and patient investigation of truth by science, which seems the very antithesis of the mystic's swift certainty, may be fostered and nourished by that very spirit of reverence in which mysticism lives and moves.*

Now whatever attitude we may take to these very general questions there is no doubt that when we read the literature of medical psychology we find that the part played by emotions or feelings in our lives is the central theme. Moreover, it is not a conflict between intellect and emotion that we there read about, but one between one emotion or impulse and another. We frequently read how the patient has 'failed to come to terms with his emotions' and how it is the duty of the physician to help him to discover the source of his conflict and to overcome it.

But not only are feelings and conflicts between them the objects with which the doctor is concerned in dealing with

* Lord Russell, 'Mysticism and Logic', *Hibbert Journal* (July 1914).

mentally sick people; the situation is further complicated by the fact that the doctor's own feelings are involved. This is another feature which puts psychological medicine in a peculiar position. In other branches it may be possible to treat the patient like an automatic machine, but this is excluded in the case of mental patients. For example, Dr A. E. Clark-Kennedy has written: 'Psychotherapy . . . demands a natural capacity for sympathetic understanding of another person's problems, which can be bred out of existence by an unbalanced scientific training.'[*] Another author writes:

The patient-physician relationship is the very core of the practice of psychiatry; it is basic in the evaluation of the patient's problems and in the appreciation of the factors that produce them; it determines the relative degree of success or failure in psychiatric treatment. In so far as physicians in general deal with sick people rather than just disease syndromes or pathology of isolated organs, the patient-physician relationship assumes an equally important role in the practice of all fields of medicine. In teaching this subject, it is important to help the student gain an understanding of the nature of this relationship, the dynamic factors in both the patient and the physician that influence it, and the manner in which an adequate relationship can be achieved.[†]

Finally we have the following full and emphatic statement of Dr D. Stafford-Clark:

At the beginning of this chapter we defined psychotherapy as a method of treatment relying for its effect upon an interchange of ideas between patient and doctor, directed towards relief of the patient's symptoms and distress. It is now time to

[*] *The Lancet*, 9 December 1950, p. 727; see also p. 763.
[†] Dr William Malamud, *Psychiatry and Medical Education*, p. 55. (Report of the 1951 Conference on Psychiatric Education held at Cornell University, Ithaca, New York.)

add that by far the most important factor in effective relief or cure, or indeed change of any kind, is the emotional quality and reality of the ideas exchanged.

A competent psychiatrist can often see in essence the core of a patient's problem by the time he has completed the preliminary study of the patient's life. Sometimes patients, sensing something of the purpose of this study, will demand an exposition of what is in the doctor's mind, in the belief or hope that this will offer them an immediate key to recovery. But in this sense unfortunately no one can learn from another's experience of his life, no matter how expert or accurate the impression formed by the doctor may prove to be.

We build up our patterns of thought and feeling slowly and often painfully, and the emotional experiences which have gone into them have to be relived rather than retold before we are liberated from their influence upon us. There is all the difference in the world between the intellectual formulation of a man's problems and personality, and that change of heart which alone can bring him release from the chains in which they may have bound him. Whether we call the link which the doctor can establish between the one and the other the transference situation or the patient-doctor relationship, we are really dealing with an emotional bond which acts as a catalyst for all the chaotic feeling and experience of the sick and unhappy person.

On the patient's side much of this emotional bond springs, as we have seen, from the reservoirs of stifled and forgotten passions; on the doctor's side from the detached but absolutely sincere and dedicated concern to help, however humbly, another human being. Behind them both there must be that greatest gift of all, the capacity to love; and for all the wisdom, skill, and technical accomplishment which ought to go into it, psychotherapy is fundamentally but another way of using the creative power of love towards the restoration of human happiness and peace of mind.*

* *Psychiatry Today* (1953), pp. 185–6. See also *A Development of the Psychoanalytical Theory and Technique of Sándor Ferenczi*, by Izette de Forest (1954).

It was pointed out in the previous section that at least two senses of 'subjective' could be distinguished. In the first sense psychology is subjective because its data involve D_2; in the second because of the difficulty of preventing scientific judgments from being warped by the personal prejudices of the investigator. It was pointed out that as far as the latter charge was concerned psychology is not alone guilty among the sciences, we were able to give examples of such subjectivity in the other sciences. In any case, as we have already pointed out in this section, this fault is not so serious as it is represented if we understand the principles of criticism of scientific statements. A little more can now be said about the first sense of 'subjective'.

It is sometimes important to distinguish three degrees so to speak of subjectivity, corresponding to the three divisions of D_2. If the reader will turn back to §7 he will see that D_2 is made up of the second domain of getting$_1$, the second domain of getting$_2$ and the second domain of getting$_3$. The second domain of getting$_3$ is distinguished from the others by the fact that it has no so-called external reference. When Tom is getting a feeling of exasperation at Molly's stubbornness this feeling is not *of* anything belonging to $D_3 - D_1$ in the same way that a view may be *of* the sea in getting$_1$. Consequently this division of D_2 (as was mentioned at the end of the last section) cannot be helped out and become interpersonal by doing, in the same way that is possible with the first division of D_2. To that extent it is more subjective than the first division. But it can still be helped out by talking and so become interpersonal.

From the learned opinions of experts which have been quoted above in this section, it is abundantly clear that medical psychology essentially involves this third division of D_2. Consequently a psychology which restricts itself to what is called overt behaviour cannot possibly do what is here required of it. The patient and the doctor are concerned with the patient's feelings as well as with his behaviour. Accordingly the purely physical training provided at present in the preclinical years in some universities, avoiding as it does the second domain of getting$_3$, is totally inadequate as a preparation for medical psychology.

We see the same failure to recognize the significance of the emotional side of life in some writings on what is called sex education. Some authors appear to believe that all that is required is a knowledge of the anatomy and physiology of the reproductive organs. They fail to see that the difficulties involved in unhappy marriages are chiefly of an emotional nature and in so far as this is the case they cannot be resolved by purely intellectual means. This is not to say that such ignorance may not be a factor and sometimes an important one in such situations. An example of the consequences of ignorance of the facts of human reproduction has already been given (p. 57).

§ 17. THE LINGUISTIC APPARATUS OF MEDICAL PSYCHOLOGY

In this section I shall bring together a somewhat miscellaneous collection of remarks about the linguistic apparatus of medical psychology. What constitutes the linguistic apparatus of this branch of science will of course be decided by medical psychologists themselves in accordance with the observations they may make and the bright ideas with which they may have the good fortune to be blessed.

But certain remarks of a general nature may not be out of place.

Pavlov and Freud, each from his own standpoint, uttered warnings against mixing psychological and neurological terminology. Each saw (more clearly than some of his followers) that if this precaution is not taken it is very easy to get into muddles and into situations in which it is very difficult to decide what precisely we are asserting with such mixed statements in the absence of any agreed criteria of meaningfulness.

But how are we to decide whether a statement is or is not one belonging to psychology? With the help of what has been said in §7 it is now possible to offer a criterion for at least some psychological statements. But I shall not claim this title for these statements, I shall content myself with calling them statements belonging to *person language*. Consider the following, for example:

(1) Tom is getting toothache by eating ice cream.
(2) Tom is falling with an acceleration of 32 feet per second per second.

Each of these statements contains a name belonging to D_1, but they differ in the following way. I can substitute for 'Tom' in (2) a name belonging to $D_3 - D_1$ and still get a statement about the meaningfulness of which there is no doubt, and one moreover which may very well be true. But if I put any name other than *the name of a person* (i.e. one belonging to D_1) for 'Tom' in (1) then I get a statement which is very difficult if not impossible to test or one which many people would say is meaningless. Thus if I put the name of someone's pet dog for 'Tom' in (1) I get a statement which is difficult to test because a dog cannot speak English (or any other human language) well enough to formulate a sentence which would be confirmatory or otherwise of the statement under discussion. If I put 'this lump of lead' for 'Tom' in (1) the result would not be a statement which anyone would wish to defend. Let us say then that in (1) a person name occurs *essentially* and that in (2) it occurs *inessentially*. Then we can say that a sentence belongs to person language if at least one person name occurs in it essentially. This would however only cover observation records or singular statements which are candidates for admission into person language. We must therefore say that a sentence belongs to person language either if at least one person name occurs in it essentially or if it is a universal or existential generalization of a sentence in which at least one person name occurs essentially. I have not called such sentences psychological statements because I do not wish to set up restrictions upon the possible ways in which it may be thought fit to construct *explanatory hypotheses* in medical psychology in the future.

The fact that person language is also part of the language of everyday life does not in any way detract from the dignity of medical psychology as a science, because all the sciences use the language of everyday life on the observational level, although this will be supplemented by technical terms as well. Neither does the fact that it belongs to the observational level mean that it is not to be taken seriously. It has been one of the principal themes of this essay that observation records and their generalizations are always to be taken *more* seriously than explanatory hypotheses, because it is by means of the former that the latter are tested and because we only use the latter to help us to get more of the former. Medical psychology is an applied science. The aim of applied science is the discovery of methods for achieving certain ends. If these methods are to be applicable they must be described in language which tells us what to say with our voices or to do with our hands and apparatus; this must therefore be language which belongs to the observational level. Explanatory hypotheses are relevant only in so far as they help us to reach statements of such a kind. This does not mean that an explanatory hypothesis which has no apparent relevance for a problem in an applied science may not be relevant at some future date. As we cannot predict the future in such matters we cannot say which explanatory hypotheses may not some day be applicable.

The statement (1) given above by way of an example of a statement belonging to person language illustrates the fact that mixed statements, i.e. statements involving both D_2 or D_1 and $D_3 - D_1$ present no difficulty *provided we remain on the observational level*. It is mixed statements on the explanatory levels which get us into difficulties.

This statement also illustrates the point that a mixed statement transcends the bounds of physics, because toothache belongs to D_2 and ice cream to $D_3 - D_1$ and the laws of physics are concerned with transactions between things all belonging to $D_3 - D_1$, but not with transactions between things belonging to $D_3 - D_1$ and those belonging to D_2 or D_1. The construction of an explanatory hypothesis of the latter type would therefore involve introducing something which is not provided for by the present hypotheses of physics. This is a point which does not appear to be very generally appreciated: either you stay within the language and laws of physics, in which case you cannot derive laws relating toothache and ice cream; or, in order to cope with laws of this kind you must introduce new explanatory hypotheses which transcend the laws and language of physics. So long as neurology operates with the neurone hypothesis within the framework of physics the theoretical task would seem to be somewhat as follows. At any given moment, in man or any other animal with central and peripheral nervous systems, torrents of impulses are assumed to be pouring into the central nervous system by the afferent neurones, and torrents of impulses are pouring out from it by the efferent neurones. The task of neurology, within such a framework, is to find a hypothesis from which it will follow that within a given time-stretch with one specific state of the afferent torrent the efferent torrent will be of one kind, and within another time-stretch with the same or a different state of the afferent torrent the efferent torrent will be of a different kind. From a strictly physical point of view any other considerations than these, coupled with hypotheses concerning states of the neurones of the central nervous system, are irrelevant. That is why, from the point of view of neurology considered as a strictly physical science (as Pavlov conceived it), mixed statements in neurology are to be avoided. Explanatory hypotheses of a mixed kind involve a radical departure from traditional methods. Whatever procedure is adopted it is difficult to see how any great progress can be expected with the very difficult tasks of neurology without extensive use of mathematics, under which I include mathematical logic. I shall return to the question of hypotheses using mixed language later, meanwhile some other topics must be dealt with.

To many people it seems obvious that psychology is a branch of biology, and if we are to classify the sciences exclusively with reference to subject-matter this view seems very plausible at first sight. Psychology investigates persons, persons are organisms, and every discipline which investigates organisms is a branch of biology, and so (it is argued) psychology must be a branch of biology. But let us not overlook the fact that although all persons are organisms, not all organisms are persons; so that the two classes are not identical and it might be said that psychology is concerned with just those aspects of persons by which they are distinguished from other organisms (especially those which involve the use of human talk). If we confine attention strictly to behaviour, described exclusively in physiological language, then the study of behaviour whether animal or human remains within the boundaries of biology. But as soon as we admit reference to D_2 (especially to its third division, the second domain of getting$_3$, which we have seen is unavoidable in medical psychology) then we leave the boundaries of biology and enter a distinct science which requires a distinct name. It has its own linguistic apparatus and its own methods of observation.* If we approach psychological problems exclusively from the biological point of view we shall miss some important facts about persons altogether. Some persons, for example, entertain and pursue certain ideals which play a great part in their lives—moral, religious, political or aesthetic ideals. Some have even laid down their lives in order not to betray their ideals. St Thomas More provides a good example. Such conduct seems quite fantastically perverse from the strictly biological point of view and cannot even be described in the language of biology. But looked at from a social point of view it is seen to have great significance. Great store is usually set upon such conduct even by the persons who do not share the ideals. This is because such ideals and such conduct concern the *quality* of life. They are of the greatest importance to the medical psychologist who has to provide for the man who hungers and thirsts after righteousness

* Each science (at a given date) is an ordered collection of statements ordered by the consequence relation. Each has its characteristic vocabulary. Whether a statement belongs to a given science depends therefore on whether it can be expressed in the existing vocabulary of that science.

as well as for the man who hungers and thirsts for beer and ham sandwiches.

Psychology has just as close, if not closer, affinities with sociology as with biology. This is particularly true of medical psychology. The doctor does not deal with patients who come to him out of a vacuum or from a desert island, but with persons who are parts in social units (e.g. families) and whose troubles have arisen as a result of these social relations. The doctor is dealing just as much with sick social units as with sick individuals; and these social units are very often sick because the persons composing them find it difficult not to be beastly to each other, or are beastly to each other without being aware of the fact.

One of the surprising things about person language is the degree to which it uses metaphors relating to D_3—D_1. We are able to understand one another with the help of such metaphors without at the same time being misled by them. This is another illustration of the point mentioned at the beginning of §7, the fact, namely, that we can often talk sense without knowing very precisely what we are talking about. For example, when we say

Tom has a cool brain and Mary has a warm heart

something tolerably definite although complicated is conveyed by this statement which would be difficult to express so briefly in any other way, although we should not attempt to test this statement by sticking a thermometer into Tom's head or Mary's thorax.

The following passage from the author's foreword to a modern novel illustrates the same point:

The idea remained *in my head* for a long time, *came forward* occasionally, and was *put back again*. I could not *make up my mind* what was the *shape* it should have. Then in 1947 I was

119

invited to the birthday party of a lady who was ninety-nine years old. She was a spry old dear, *clear-headed*, and I talked to her of many things, and felt a sense of awe when I thought of the *backward reach* of her mind.*

This passage illustrates the fact that person language as it exists embedded in a natural language does not recognize atopical relations (see p. 64) and so treats them as spatial relations. This is at the root of many of these metaphors. When we use these metaphors not only do we (in a sense) not know what we are talking about but we say what we do not mean in order to convey what we do mean. But this state of affairs is not confined to psychology. It prevails in various ways and to various degrees in other sciences. Sentences like

it reddens circularly

seem to be non-metaphorical, but

Tom is black

is perhaps metaphorical in the sense of the *Shorter Oxford English Dictionary*, which says: ' *Metaphor*. The figure of speech in which a name or descriptive term is transferred to some object to which it is not properly applicable.' Of course everything depends here upon how we interpret 'properly applicable'. For some scientific purposes it might be desirable to say that 'black' is not properly applicable to Tom but only to views of Tom, and that it is only secondarily or derivatively applicable to Tom, although in ordinary conversation we should say that it was properly applicable to Tom. In the first case we could say that 'black' was a name which is transferred to some object to which it is not properly applicable and so is metaphorically used. Only if the views of Tom are parts

* Howard Spring, *The Houses in Between* (1951). Italic not in text.

of him can we say that no such transference has occurred. On the other hand

Tom has two legs

is not metaphorical because, although we have to get a view or a feel of Tom in order to discover whether we agree with this statement, we do not wish to say that the view or the feel we get has two legs, but only that we get a view or a feel of two legs.

In the case of explanatory hypotheses we are being metaphorical when we think of hypothetical entities after the pattern of things belonging to $D_3 - D_1$, as when atoms are thought of as miniature solar systems. With explanatory hypotheses such imagery seems strictly speaking to be irrelevant, although it may be helpful, up to a point, for teaching purposes. What is required of a good explanatory hypothesis is that it should have among its consequences the zero-level statements which suggested it in the first instance, as well as other unexpected consequences which will stimulate further investigation. It should not require too much bolstering up by the explaining away of unfavourable observation records. What imagery people may get when they think about a hypothesis seems to be of little importance. What is important is the structure of the hypothesis. It was pointed out above that the consequence relation depends not on the subject-matter but on the structure of the sentences concerned. With these points in mind we can consider the following remarks about some notions that have appeared in explanatory hypotheses of medical psychology. The first is in a passage from the book by Professor Notcutt which has already been mentioned; he is referring to psychoanalysis:

In the later analytical writings, all descriptions of defence mechanisms are phrased in terms of ego, id and super-ego, so that it becomes hard to explain their meaning in other terms. Psycho-analysis is firmly committed to the acceptance of the three little men inside your head who deceive one another, quarrel and make friends again, form alliances, offer bribes, and shut a knowing eye to an indiscretion. Often there seems to be only a vague recollection that these are metaphors whose proper field of application is a very restricted one, and there is a danger of making an Athanasian mystery out of a useful distinction.*

The next passage is from an article by Professor C. A. Mace:

A conception of this sort was first presented in a fairly detailed way in Bishop Butler's *Sermons on Human Nature*. Butler describes human nature as a three-tiered hierarchy. At the base of the pyramid lie the particular impulses; at the second level the two regulative principles of Cool Self-love and Benevolence; and at the apex the supreme controlling agent Conscience. The schema is reproduced with remarkable fidelity in the system of McDougall with his three-tiered hierarchy of instincts, sentiments and the master sentiment of Self Regard. Nor is the pattern very different in Freud, who has his own three-tiered hierarchy of Id, Ego and Super-ego. If McDougall may be described as Butler in modern dress, Freud might be described as Butler in fancy dress. But the analogies though instructive must not be pressed too far.†

Finally, Dr George Day has discussed a tripartite doctrine of Psyche, Pneuma and Soma which, as he points out, recalls Plato's analogy of the charioteer and his two horses—one well behaved and the other unruly.‡

It was pointed out in §4 that the introduction of an explanatory hypothesis involves *changing the subject*. In our present context this means *ceasing to talk about the person under consideration and talking about something else*. In

* *The Psychology of Personality* (1953), p. 131.

† 'Homeostasis, needs and values', *British Journal of Psychology* (general section), vol. XLIV (1953), p. 201.

‡ The Hunterian Society Oration delivered on Monday, 25 February 1952. Reported in *The Lancet*, 11 October 1952, p. 694.

principle there would appear to be three ways of changing the subject. First we may talk about something of which the subject in question is a part. This is what happens in astronomy. Next we can talk about the parts of the subject as when atoms are thought of as miniature solar systems. Thirdly we can speak of things which are atopically related to our original subject. This third alternative seems to be the one followed in psychology. Instead of talking about Tom and his doings we talk about entities which appear to be atopically related to Tom and are spoken of as though they were among his possessions, thus in Freud's case we have Tom's id, his ego and his super-ego.* We also notice the striking *structural* resemblance between the hypotheses of Butler, Freud, McDougall and Day, which is seen in the tripartite division which each requires, and in the fact that in each case two of the terms exert pressure (metaphorically speaking) in different directions (again metaphorically!) whilst a third tries to reconcile them. If medical men have found hypotheses of this type helpful in their dealings with patients, then such hypotheses are surely deserving of our respect, and we should not allow ourselves to be diverted from them by jests (and metaphorical ones at that) about 'three little men inside your head'. Such imagery is quite irrelevant to the success of the hypothesis, even more so here than it is in other sciences. Let us rather be thankful for *any* hypotheses in this field. If we are too fussy about their metaphorical character at the present stage of the development of medical psychology we may be in danger of damming up all hypotheses at the source.

Similar misunderstandings also occur in connexion with

---

* Id, ego and super-ego appear to be thought of as persons 'composing' Tom in an atopical sense. If that is the case, their place is in that part of D_1 which is outside D_3.

explanatory hypotheses which attempt to connect psychology with neurology and to which we have already briefly referred in the present section. There is, for example, the well-known saying of Charles Mercier: 'Try to imagine the idea of a beefsteak binding the molecules [of the brain] together. It is impossible.' Sir Russell Brain has recently asked: 'Can we imagine how the passage of electrical impulses along certain nerve fibres to an end-station in the brain can result in a sensation of pain?'*

To imagine something is to get a view or a sound or something else belonging to D_2 which is *of* it in the sense of getting$_2$. But molecules and electrical impulses do not belong to D_3 and therefore have no views, sounds, etc. We cannot therefore imagine them, but this does not prevent us from trying to construct sentences which have among their consequences statements about things belonging to D_2 as well as statements containing such notions as 'brain molecule' and 'neural impulse', which is what we must do if we want to have explanatory hypotheses of the kind in question. What we can or cannot imagine is irrelevant to this problem. There seem to be no obstacles, except human infirmity, to the construction of hypotheses having the right structure to accomplish such tasks, which at the same time are purely abstract or formal in the sense that no sort of imagery is connected with them. But they must satisfy the requirement that, in conjunction with other statements of the theory in which they occur, some of their consequences will belong to zero-level and can therefore be challenged by observation records. In this connexion the following passage by the nineteenth-century mathematician, A. B. Kempe, is worth pondering upon:

* *Mind, Perception and Science* (1951), p. 66. For recent attempts to construct psycho-physical hypotheses see R. O. Kapp, *Mind, Life and Body* (1951); and J. C. Eccles, *The Neurophysiological Basis of Mind* (1953).

Whatever may be the true nature of things and of the conceptions which we have of them, in the operations of reasoning they are dealt with as a number of separate entities or units, some units are distinguished from one another and some are not. Each of the forms which a system of any number of units can assume, owing to varieties of distribution, is one of a definite number of possible forms, and the peculiarities and properties of the collection depend, as far as the processes of reasoning are concerned, upon the particular form it assumes, and are independent of the dress in which it is presented; so that two systems which are of the same form have precisely the same properties, although the garbs in which they are severally clothed may lead us to place the systems under very different categories, and even to regard them as belonging to different branches of science.

When people complain that they find certain words which occur in psychological literature unintelligible, we must explain to them the distinction between being intelligible in the sense of being imaginable and being intelligible in the subtler sense of occurring in an explanatory hypothesis which has testable consequences.

We can distinguish between what is commonly called the *extension* of a name and what I shall call its *specification*. The extension is the class or set of all the things to which the name applies. Thus the extension of 'cow' is the class of all cows; past, present or to come. The name 'cow' can also on occasion be used to designate the class of cows itself, although this is not a cow! Thus the sentences 'Mary is a cow', 'Mary belongs to the class of cows', 'Mary is a member of the class cow', ' "cow" names Mary' or 'Mary satisfies a specification of "cow" ', are all different ways of conveying the same information.

On the other hand a specification of the word 'cow' is what you have to know in order to be able to use the word correctly. I say 'a specification' rather than 'the specification' because a name can have two or more distinct specifications all corresponding to the same extension.

A name can have a specification although its extension is null or empty, as is commonly assumed to be the case with 'mermaid' the specification of which is: 'chordate animal the anterior half of which is that of a woman whilst the posterior half is that of a fish.'

Many names occurring in the high-level hypotheses of natural science may or may not have a non-empty extension according to whether the explanatory hypothesis is true. But as we cannot know whether an explanatory hypothesis is true we cannot know whether the extension of a name occurring in it is empty or not. Such names frequently have no specification but are meaningful only by virtue of the testability of the sentences in which they occur. What is often called 'demonstrating' things named by such names consists in setting up an experiment which shows a result which is confirmatory of a prediction made with the help of the hypothesis.

We use vast numbers of names in daily life without being able to specify them verbally. Suppose the word 'fouy' occurs in a theory of natural science and someone asks us what it means, what possible procedures are open to us? If, which is unlikely, 'fouy' names something in D_2 then you must so arrange matters that your questioner *gets* a fouy; and you must say to him: 'What you are now getting is a fouy.' But you must take care that he understands to which, of the many things he is getting at the time, you are referring; and you must take care that he is not deaf or colour blind, etc., as the case may require.

If a fouy is a member of D_3 you can put a fouy into your questioner's hands and say: 'That is a fouy.' Or, if that is impossible on account of size or distance, you must take him to a place where there are fouys and say: 'You are now getting a view (or sound, or feel, or smell, etc.) of a fouy.'

This method has its difficulties and drawbacks. One demonstration is usually not enough. If someone wanted to know what a person was and you pointed to a man about to jump off a spring board into a swimming pool, the questioner might get the impression that the word 'person' applied only to scantily dressed men. But even if you pointed out a great variety of human beings, men, women and children, in all varieties of occupation, etc., you still might fail to give your questioner an adequate notion of what 'person' means. This is because he would only be getting views, sounds, feels, etc., of persons. The best answer would be: 'You are a person.'

Another method of indicating the extension of a word or other sign is that followed in this essay in explaining D_1, D_2 and D_3, namely by taking statements which occur in everyday life, like:

Tom is getting a view of the sea from his bedroom window

which it is hoped will easily be understood, and asking the reader to apply the label 'D_1' to things whose names can be substituted for 'Tom' without making the sentence meaningless; and so on for the other expressions. Finally there is the method of strict definition in which we seek to construct, out of words already familiar to the reader, what is in effect a compound name having the same extension as the name to be defined.

If in connexion with the foregoing remarks about the specification of names the reader notes the following sentence from a passage in the British Medical Association's Report on the medical curriculum, extracts of which have already been quoted above, 'The student should also be disciplined in the proper use and meaning of words and the relationship of names and words to ideas and things', he will see how much is being required of the student and how complicated this question is.

In considering how a statement in medical psychology is to be formulated, careful consideration should be given to the question whether a notion should be introduced in substantival, adjectival, adverbial or verbal form. Because the more we admit in substantival form the more we may be in danger of that multiplication of entities beyond necessity against which we have frequently been warned.* Sir Ernest Gowers writes:

Abstract nouns are indispensable in their proper places. But one of the greatest faults of present-day writing is to use them to excess. There are two reasons why this is bad. First, it means that statements are made in a roundabout instead of a direct way, and the meaning is more difficult to grasp. The commonest form of roundabout is to make an abstract noun the subject of a sentence which would be clear and more natural if its subject were a concrete noun or a personal pronoun. . . . Secondly, abstract nouns have less precise meanings than concrete ones, and therefore should be avoided as far as possible by those who wish to make their meaning plain.†

The author then gives many examples from official and business writing of the misuse of abstract nouns. To these I would add the following:

(1) The movement of Tom is rapid.
(2) The rapidity of Tom's movement is surprising.
(3) Your surprise at the rapidity of Tom's movement is understandable.

* See the remarks about 'substance' in § 10, p. 65 above.
† *A B C of Plain Words* (1951), p. 1.

Actually these do not present any great obscurity, unless we pause over them and demand that there should be 'entities' corresponding to such nouns as 'movement' and 'rapidity'. I mention these examples merely to show how easy it is to avoid such nouns.

(1) Tom is moving rapidly.
(2) Tom is moving surprisingly rapidly.
(3) I also am surprised that Tom is moving so rapidly.

Coming to more specifically psychological matters we can contrast the two following major types of formulation:

I.

Tom {
  { urged on / impelled / buoyed up / motivated } by the { wish / desire / hope / aim } to get / of getting { married next year }
  { entertains / has set himself } the { intention / aim }
}

II.

Tom { wishes / desires / hopes / intends / aims at getting } to get married next year

If we adopt the first set of formulations, we shall have things like wishes, hopes, desires, aims, etc., on our hands; or so it may seem, and these do not appear to fit into any of our three fundamental domains of getting. But by the simple device of adopting the second set of formulations this difficulty can—if that is desired—be completely avoided.

There is an ambiguity connected with the use of the ubiquitous verb 'to be' which is relevant to our present topic. Sometimes, as when we say

Paris is the capital of France,

we use 'is' in the sense of 'is identical with'. We mean that the name to the left of 'is' and the phrase to the right of it both apply to one and the same thing. But when we say that Tom is a skinful of chemicals or that he is a cluster of miniature billiard balls we are asserting that certain of the explanatory hypotheses of chemistry and physics are applicable to Tom. But we are not using 'is' in the sense of 'is identical with' because, as we have seen, there are things we want to say about Tom which we can express in person language but which we should not classify as laws of chemistry or of physics. It is this which distinguishes $D_1 . D_3$ from $D_3 - D_1$.

The medical psychologist is not quite so free as his colleague in pure psychology in his choice of language and explanatory hypotheses. From what was said in the last section it is clear that language which has a depersonalizing effect would be harmful to the doctor-patient relationship. This is also responsible for the objection that some patients feel at being treated as automatic machines waiting for the penny to drop. But we have seen that passing to an explanatory hypothesis involves changing the subject, and if this means ceasing to talk about persons then talk involving such a hypothesis might have a depersonalizing effect. Such difficulties will be avoided if the doctor is not misled regarding the status of explanatory hypothesis and is careful not to mix technical jargon appropriate to such hypotheses with the person language with which he will ordinarily communicate with his patients. Actually, the psychological hypotheses to which reference has been made in this section do not involve depersonalization; they simply give separate names to distinct impulses or tendencies of the one person.

Other issues—especially those connected with religion and morals, which do not arise in physical medicine—also seem to be unavoidable in medical psychology. Dr E. B. Strauss, in his presidential address to the Section of Psychiatry of the Royal Society of Medicine, entitled 'Moral responsibility and the Law',* after saying that the title 'will immediately cause discomfort in the minds of those psychiatrists who believe that a psychiatrist should be so detached from a philosophy of values and from moral considerations of all kinds as to be able to practise his art and science in a kind of moral vacuum', adds:

Nevertheless, it has always been my contention that no doctor (whether he practises psychological medicine or any other branch) can afford to adopt a position of such artificial isolation without running the risk of losing touch with reality.

In the physical sciences moral considerations do not arise; neither do they in the science of persons so long as we are not concerned with *applying* them to persons. But as soon as we enter the field of applied science the situation is different. In applied science we propose to *do* something, so that human conduct is involved, and as soon as human conduct is involved moral questions will arise, such as: ought the doctor to do this? Ought the patient to do that? and if so what effect will the treatment have upon his attitude towards such action? Now medicine is an applied science and therefore it seems clear that Dr Strauss is correct in maintaining that it is not possible to shut your eyes to moral problems, especially in psychological medicine. It also seems clear that every psychological

* *Proceedings of the Royal Society of Medicine*, vol. 47 (1954), p. 41.

hypothesis which is only tenable if the distinction between 'doing it on purpose' and 'doing it because you couldn't help it' is explained away as an illusion of common sense will, if employed in psychological medicine, expose the doctor to the risks of the 'artificial isolation' to which Dr Strauss refers. Moreover, a mode of treatment which resulted in the patient no longer wishing to live would produce a situation comparable to that mentioned in Dickens, of the father who 'cut his little boy's head off to cure him of squinting'.

I should like to urge that the doctor should not let his attitude to morals and religion be too much influenced by the success of the physical sciences, but that a more tolerant and broadminded attitude is called for. In so far as it is a doctor's business to guide and help rather than to preach or judge, it is difficult to see how any other kind of attitude will serve his ends.

The main issue can perhaps be expressed in the following way. Should we continue in the present prevailing habit of taking D_3 realistically and D_1 sceptically, always assuming that anything we may discover about persons which is expressed in D_1 language can be expressed in D_3 language if we try hard enough, *or* should we entertain the possibility of taking D_1 seriously in its own right, as an uncharted ocean requiring its own methods of exploration, its own linguistic apparatus, and its own criteria of success? I am not at all advocating the view that D_1 should be taken dogmatically and D_3 sceptically. This was perhaps the attitude of Sir Arthur Eddington when he wrote: 'In comparing the certainty of things spiritual and things temporal, let us not forget this—Mind is the first and most direct thing in our experience; all else is remote inference.'*

* *Science and the Unseen World* (1929), p. 24.

There is no certainty either of things spiritual or of things temporal, otherwise there would be no need for faith. The notion of mind, like the notions of self, soul and spirit, are notions concerned with D_1, just as the notion of physical things is concerned with D_3. But none of these things can be said to be 'in our experience' in the sense in which the things of D_2 are 'in our experience'. It seems equally unfortunate to speak here of 'inference'. All these notions, whether they relate to D_1 or to D_3, have presumably arisen and survived because they are helpful in some way, enabling us to talk in situations in which we should otherwise be compelled to remain silent. But none of these notions has been reached by inference; we find ourselves in possession of them as soon as we begin to reflect. About their origin in ourselves or others we can only make hypotheses, and such hypotheses are always difficult to test.

Fundamentally then, as far as how we come by them is concerned, the notions belonging to D_1 and those belonging to D_3 are all on the same footing. It is not a question of the former being reached by something called 'faith' and the latter by something called 'reason'; faith and reason are required for both. But the things belonging to D_3 have the great advantage already noted that some objects of D_2 are *of* them, and these objects of D_2 can frequently, without great harm, be treated *as if* they *were* the physical objects themselves. Coupled with this is *doing* in relation to D_3. All this greatly helps to make concrete the physical world and makes doubt, not belief, regarding it difficult. Moreover D_3 enjoys all the advantages which depend on its association with successful physical science and its resulting prestige. When we turn to D_1 we find none of these advantages. We find ourselves entangled in the still unresolved antithesis of heart and head. We know about the special peculiarities of persons not so much by the views, etc., which we get of them as by *being* persons ourselves. This vivid but elusive awareness becomes in some measure objectified by talk, but in so far as the available linguistic apparatus is so much less perfect than that available for D_3 in just so far will the process of objectification also be less perfect. Here again the language of D_1 suffers on account of its former incorrect association with D_3. It is difficult to speak of 'the things of the spirit' because in the vocabulary of D_3 'spirit' is only admitted if it is preceded by 'methylated' or some such word. What is wanted is a linguistic apparatus which will enable us to talk as easily, naturally and successfully about D_1 as the physical-object language enables us to talk about D_3. This does not at all mean that the former must be modelled on the latter. The D_1 language will have affinities with literature such as the D_3 language cannot have. Successful talk will bring faith with it. But there must also be faith that the task of exploring what is at first a mere possibility is worth doing. A sincere sceptic who insisted on 'living by the light of reason' alone would soon die of starvation, waiting for his food to be chemically analysed to ensure that it did not poison him. But even this would not suffice, because it would (contrary to his principles) involve the belief that the general chemical laws upon which the tests were based held good also in the particular case of their application to his food.

The great objection to adopting the usual view that the methods and hypotheses appropriate to D_3 are all that we need and that it is a waste of time to try anything else, is that it shuts, bolts and bars the door to developments in any direction but one. The second alternative would be to entertain the hypothesis that we are in the same stage in relation to D_1 as were the predecessors of Galileo in relation to D_3. We may have everything to learn about it both as regards methods and linguistic apparatus. It might be objected to this that if such possibilities were admitted we should let in at the same time a host of charlatans, magicians and other arrant knaves. The answer to this is simple. Look back again to the beginnings of the physical sciences. The stimulus to their development came, not so much from white-robed philosophers with clear and critical intellects who did not like to get their fingers dirty, as from the 'sooty empirics' who laboured in the workshops of alchemists, hunting for the elixir of life, the philosopher's stone, and other disreputable things. These men followed their naïve beliefs about the physical world and thought it worthy of their attention. If they had not so believed, the physical sciences would presumably never have been set upon their triumphal path. Methods of investigation and of criticism, and appreciation of the criteria of success, develop gradually in the course of the work; they are not given from the start. The second alternative thus encourages the thought that the future may still have something exciting in store for us, and may show us that the poets and prophets, the mystics and martyrs are not simply misguided enthusiasts after all, but have something important to teach us.*

* For further reading in connexion with this section the reader may be recommended to consult the volume entitled *Selected Papers on Philosophy* by William James in the Everyman Library; IX and X of I. D. Suttie's *Origins of Love and Hate* (1935); J. A. Hadfield, *Psychology and Morals*; L. D. Weatherhead, *Psychology, Religion and Healing* (1952); the articles, 'Faith and health', by R. W. Luxton, *The Lancet*, 21 August 1954, p. 379, and 'Mental health and spiritual values', by Sir Geoffrey Vickers, *The Lancet*, 12 March 1955, p. 521. The reader who wishes to exercise his capacity for broad-mindedness will find ample opportunity in many of the items of the extensive bibliography of E. Underhill's *Mysticism* (1942).

§ 18. SUMMARY

It would be difficult to summarize the somewhat long and rather complicated argument of this essay, but it has already been partly summarized in §12; the points which I would wish to emphasize in conclusion are the following. In the early days of physics it was necessary to exclude the notion of person from science because in the province of physics it was not applicable. The resulting success of the physical sciences has not unnaturally had the effect of swinging the pendulum of opinion to the opposite extreme of excluding this notion from science permanently, even from the science of persons itself. In the above pages I have pleaded for the recognition of the autonomy of the sciences and for a rejection of the claim that everything has been discovered 'in principle', so that all we need to do now is to settle down, with our well-established methods, to working out the details. In opposition to this view (which involves being permanently contented with a particular system of explaining away) I have urged that the proper understanding of D_1 has hardly begun, that both as regards methods, ideas and hypotheses we seem to have an enormous amount to learn, and that the required new methods and ideas, when we free ourselves sufficiently from the old ones to be able to find them, may well be very strange and surprising from the point of view of orthodox physical science. It may even require unexpected changes in our attitude towards our linguistic apparatus in science, although such changes are not altogether unprovided for by modern researches into the role of language in science. These possibilities have been mentioned not because the methods of the physical sciences have at all exhausted their usefulness, but because, as we saw in §6, their very success necessarily shuts the door on other possible methods and channels of investigation, and so deprives us of any surprises that these may have in store for us.

The medical investigator who wishes to take a more comprehensive view of his task than that suggested by his present curriculum, and one more appropriate to the present high percentage of mentally sick patients, will, it is hoped, be helped by what has been said here about the three domains of getting, and by an understanding of the distinction between generalizations of observation records and explanatory hypotheses, which has here been explained at some length. This will arm him for his task of study and research in medical psychology by helping him to resist too much pressure from physical hypotheses, especially when these have insufficient footing in psychological observation, or can only maintain themselves by recourse to the process of explaining away. Let us hope that understanding these things will also be a stimulus to challenging and synthesizing existing hypotheses in medical psychology. Explanatory hypotheses are devices for exhibiting the complexity of nature as though it were simple; in preserving a critical attitude towards them we are therefore following the advice of A. N. Whitehead when he wrote:

Should we not distrust the jaunty assurance with which every age prides itself that it at last has hit upon the ultimate concepts in which all that happens can be formulated? The aim of science is to seek the simplest explanations of complex facts. We are apt to fall into the error of thinking that the facts are simple because simplicity is the goal of our quest. The guiding motto in the life of every natural philosopher should be Seek simplicity and distrust it.*

* *The Concept of Nature* (1926), p. 163.

POSTSCRIPT

WHILE this book was going through the press an article appeared in *The Lancet* (10 December 1955, pp. 1203–8) which illustrates many of the points which have been discussed above. The author, S. A. Barnett, urges the application of certain notions which have been developed in ethology (the scientific study of animal behaviour) to problems of psycho-somatic disorder. But he also makes a number of important pronouncements on theoretical matters and on the linguistic apparatus of psychology from the same standpoint, which come within the scope of this essay. He believes that the present terminologies of psychologists and psychiatrists are often a handicap to progress. He finds that 'the gulfs between psychiatry, psychology, ethology and physiology are both wide and deep, and the attempt to bridge them is liable to bring on a fit of dizziness'. He believes that 'an urgent necessity is for those who practise one discipline to learn the language of the others'. Nevertheless, he is careful to add: 'It is not suggested for a moment that only doctors use imprecise or obscurantist terminologies.' One point, therefore, which this author wishes to maintain is that the language of psychology is imprecise in the sense that it is by no means clear what psychologists are talking about. But it may be well to recall (see p. 39 above) that it is often the case that we do not know what we are talking about in science. What is important is that our talk should be *successful*, and, as the history of science shows, scientific talk has often been successful when the people who did the talking did not know what they were talking about. For example, in the early days of the differential calculus people thought that when they used it they were talking about things called infinitesimals. Later, when the doctrine of limits was worked out, the notion of infinitesimals was dropped and not used again. And so, from the point of view of the doctrine of limits, the early users of the differential calculus did not know what they were talking about. But this did not at all prevent their talk from being successful in mechanics.

Regarding bridging gulfs it should be noticed that most of the disciplines mentioned by Barnett are still in an early stage of development. In that case the attempt to build bridges between them may well be premature, because bridging gulfs here means finding very general hypotheses from which the statements (or some of them) belonging to the several disciplines follow; and these will be relatively high-level hypotheses which may be very difficult to find at present. Bridging two disciplines should not be confused with one discipline being ingested by another.

Barnett insists that the terminologies and interpretations of psychologists and psychiatrists 'should be strictly monistic'. He says: 'one fundamental conclusion arises from the argument presented here—that a monistic frame of reference is the only one which satisfies the need of communication about behaviour'. What does he mean by 'monistic'? This term is commonly applied to certain metaphysical doctrines, what can it mean in a scientific context? It is clear from what he says that the author means that we should abandon talk about D_1 and restrict ourselves to D_3, the things of D_2 being regarded as by-products of certain neural events belonging to D_3 or of hypothetical events suggested by the study of D_3. It is also clear from all that he says that he wishes to urge psychologists and psychiatrists to adopt this attitude. Now this view may well suffice for the needs of students of animal behaviour because sub-human animals cannot talk human languages. But as we have pointed out above (see especially § 16, pp. 106 *et seq.*), as soon as we deal with persons a new source of information is open to us: we know about persons so to speak at first hand, by *being* persons; part of what we get is *of* ourselves and yet is not got by seeing, feeling, hearing, tasting or smelling (cf. p. 112). Moreover, we can in some measure communicate or objectify this special information because we can talk to each other about it. Thus the relation between doctor and patient has features which are not found in the relation between bird-watcher and herring gull.

When Barnett speaks of exponents of these various related disciplines learning each others' languages, what he really recommends is that they should all learn to talk the language of ethology and should abandon their own. He writes: 'It is assumed that the aim of ethology, of which psychology is a part, is the fullest possible understanding and consequently prediction and control, of behaviour.' But, as we have just seen, you cannot express *all* you want to say about persons in the language of ethology because its vocabulary is not big enough, and so psychology cannot be a part of ethology (cf. pp. 112 and 117). It would be more feasible to treat ethology as a part of psychology if one *must* be a part of the other. What is more important at present is that each should be free to decide what it wants to say and how it should say it, and not allow itself to be dictated to by any other science. If some psychologists find it helpful in some circumstances to use such words as 'mind', 'soul' or 'spirit' (in the non-alcoholic sense), it is not a valid objection to say that they (still less that you) do not know what they mean by them. Neither is it a valid objection to say that they must not be used because they are not monistic. As regards the 'prediction and control' referred to in the passage quoted above, it should be remembered that the aim of psycho-therapy is not to give the physician control over his patient (e.g. as in successful hypnosis), but to restore the patient's control over himself.

If this author's advice were followed by psychologists and psychiatrists, it would mean the complete abandon-ment of person language and of all hope of improving it for medical purposes (see above pp. 37 and 70). The author himself is aware of a difficulty here. He says: 'the way of speaking adopted here is, to some people, distasteful and even odious: to them it seems inhuman' and he adds: 'This attitude deserves respect, since it often reflects a real and necessary concern with the needs of the whole human personality. The question remains, however, whether the formulations suggested in this paper help towards the successful application of knowledge to human ends. The ends to which knowledge is put depend on the motivation of scientists, physicians, and others, not on their prose style.' This passage contains two points of great interest and importance. First it is interesting to note that the author himself abandons the language of ethology and talks that of human or personal psychology; he does this for the simple reason that the language of ethology could not cope with what he wants to say. The second point is that persons differ quite a lot in their ends and a given theory or way of talking may favour one type of end rather than another.

As far as physicians are concerned we know what these ends are: they are the restoration of sick persons to health. If a doctrine which involves treating persons like robots (as a purely ethological theory does) leads to the restora-tion of health, it will be successful and therefore adopted. But a method may well succeed with some persons and fail with others. It was pointed out above (p. 4) that some patients resent being treated like robots. In English-speaking countries, and in many of those in which more than one political party is permitted, people have a strong dislike of having their behaviour controlled by others. Again, on a purely ethological basis, what becomes of the doctor-patient relationship about which so much has been said? It becomes an encounter between two robots and, in view of what was said above on p. 110, this may not be favourable from a psychotherapeutic point of view.

But when we consider other human ends and motivation we see that Barnett's proposals, if taken seriously, have still wider implications. It is difficult, for example, to see how it leaves any room for religion or for moral responsibility. Yet some people are religious and some believe in moral responsibility. If they fall sick, a method of treatment which conflicts with their deepest needs and convictions may well be unsuccessful, however successful it may be with others. The point of view advocated in the article under discussion will therefore appeal to, and perhaps be successfully applicable to, only certain types of patient. It should, for example, appeal strongly to Marxists and to people who hold related beliefs. It takes us some considerable way along the road to the Brave New World of Aldous Huxley and the 1984 of George Orwell. For those to whom this is a consummation devoutly to be wished, the author's doctrine will be welcome, but to many whose tastes do not lie in such directions the opposite will be the case. For this and other reasons already explained in this essay it seems to me that the author claims too much. It is not difficult to imagine the cries of protest and indignation which would go up from many quarters if an attempt were made to impose upon medical

psychology a doctrine which would be perfectly satisfactory to patients who were, let us say, devout Roman
Catholics, but to few others. But when a doctrine is proposed for medical psychology which will be perfectly
satisfactory to Marxists but to few others, little or no
protest is made. This may be because it is cloaked in the
language of the successful and respectable physical
sciences, and its more remote political and theological
implications are not at once appreciated. But surely
medicine should be neutral in these matters and offer its
helping hand to all and sundry, irrespective of creed or
politics. And if this is so it must be shy of adopting any
doctrine which will restrict its hypothesis-making and
modes of treatment to one particular theoretical direction.

It is becoming recognized that what develops from an
egg depends both on the kind of egg it is and on the kind
of environment in which it develops, so that a classification of what are called characters into hereditary (dependent on the kind of egg) and acquired (dependent on
the kind of environment) is silly. Let us hope that before
long it will be recognized that all human illness has two
aspects which we cannot separate and neither of which,
even in the most 'physical' of illnesses, can be totally
ignored with safety.*

*See D. Stafford Clark, *Psychiatry Today* (1953), p. 235.

INDEX